FINISHING STRONG

Overcoming to Fulfill Your Destiny

John W. Shuey

Cover design by: Todd Gearhart
Printed in the United States of America

CONTENTS

FOREWORD

It's a question which has been central to the human experience since before the days of Job: *Why would a loving God permit suffering in the world if He has the means to put an end to it?* You'll be hard pressed to find anyone who hasn't had this question press them into a deeper level of honesty with God about their own grief, and you'll not find a pastor who hasn't spent sleepless nights asking God for words of comfort to help make sense of a parishioner's suffering. Many an atheist will cite this as their reason for their unbelief, and many a solid believer have had their faith pressed to its limits by the nagging question about the authenticity of God's love in the midst of pain.

There have been a great number of works written on the subject by some of the greatest minds and hearts in Christendom. And while answers for the mind offer only a small comfort for a heart broken by pain and suffering, it is good to find the peace provided by God's Word -- before and during times of hardship. As the writers of Hebrews put it: *"This hope we have as an anchor of the soul, a hope both sure and steadfast and one which enters within the veil, where Jesus has entered as a forerunner for us..."* (Hebrews 6:19-20a)

John Shuey is a friend, a co-laborer, and one of the most apt teachers of the word I have had the privilege of knowing in my years of pastoral ministry. In this latest book, *Finishing* Strong, He has offered us a simple, straightforward, and heartfelt exhortation on a difficult subject. With his characteristic simplicity, making things simple which we have made complex, John has done a masterful job at digging into what the scriptures have to say on this subject. He has peppered his work with real-life stories of persecuted and other suffering believers, who have applied the Word of God to their situations and have come through victorious.

I pray you will be encouraged as you read, and will do the same!

Pastor Steve Blayer
Millersburg, PA

INTRODUCTION

God's plan has always been to bring everything together under Jesus Christ (Ephesians 1:9-10). He had planned since the beginning of creation to use the humans He had placed upon the earth to take His rule throughout the earth (Genesis 1:26-28). The first humans, however, decided that they wanted to act independently from God, which sent both the human race and the world spirally out of control in the opposite direction.

God never gave up on His plan. When things got really bad, God decided to start over with the family of Noah, a righteous man (Genesis 6-9). Again, humans rebelled against God, and they decided to pact together in order to rebel against God's command to fill the entire earth. This time, God confused their languages, which thrust them throughout the earth connecting only with those who spoke the same language as they did.

Finally, God called Abraham. He told Abraham that He would bless all families of the earth through his descendants (Genesis 12:1-3). God intended that the blessing would flow through the Jewish people, who were descendants of Abraham's son Isaac. Although the Jewish people had an" on-again, off-again relationship with God, God remained faithful to the Jewish people, continually promising that He would send a Messiah to bless them and every people on earth.

Finally, in the fullness of time, the Messiah came to earth. Jesus Christ is the Messiah! The very Son of God became man and became the Savior of the world. While He lived on earth, He lived a sinless life, trained the future leaders of the church, died on the cross to pay for the sins of all mankind and rose from the grave to provide a new life for all who receive Him as Lord and Savior. Just before Jesus went back to be with His Father, He told His disciples, and all those who would come after them, to make disciples in all nations (every ethnic group) in the world. He wants His people to go to every part of the world, make disciples, and bring every place under the control of Jesus.

After they were empowered by the Holy Spirit, the disciples began to produce more disciples who, in turn, began to reach peoples from various parts of the known world.

They had great successes, but they also began to experience hardship and suffering, as they moved from place to place proclaiming the Good News of Jesus. Immediately, they faced opposition from religious leaders. They were taken in for questioning, thrown in prison, told not to preach about Jesus, and killed for their faith.

At other times, they faced shipwreck, disease, financial difficulties and the attraction of the world. Any of these would be enough to cause discouragement, which would cause them to back off from their quest to fulfill God's Great Commission. But Jesus desired for His disciples to keep moving forward by continuing to advance His Kingdom. He told them that anyone who began to plow and looked back is not fit for His Kingdom (Luke 9:62). Jesus makes it clear that even when we face resistance or hardship, He calls us to *keep plowing* like He did.

Finishing Strong has been written to help Christ's disciples to keep plowing even when faced with great difficulties. There are two major sections to *Finishing Strong*, designed to address two issues:

<u>Section One</u> (Chapters 1-4) helps believers understand that hardships do happen to believers. This section has not been designed to cause discouragement. It is written to bring encouragement.

<u>Chapter One</u> describes the life that God wants each of us to

live. It is an amazing life filled with peace, joy and purpose. Chapter 1 has been written to present what God desires, what can be, in order to motivate us to keep plowing when the going gets tough.

<u>Chapter Two</u> discusses people in the Bible who faced difficulty. It describes some who did not finish strong, and others who kept plowing and accomplished great things for God in their generation. It shows us that we can make it because others have gone through their whole life walking in faithfulness to God. It challenges us to be like them!

<u>Chapters Three and Four</u> talk about the types of suffering that we may experience and the sources of that suffering.

We have spent this much time on this subject because some people may believe that now that they have become a Christian, everything will run smoothly all the time. There are even those out there who teach us that Christians should always be healthy and wealthy. If we believe that everything should be perfect all the time, we will be shocked when difficulty comes. We may even become disillusioned or angry with God. When this happens, we may quit serving God or drastically back off in our passion for Him. If we know that we may face resistance and other obstacles, we will not be shocked and will look to God to assist us to wend our way through. Please keep reading. These chapters are informative, but will provide teaching to help us keep plowing.

<u>Section Two</u> (Chapters Five through Thirteen) shows us the help God has provided to assist us to keep moving forward, even when we are rocked with hardships.

<u>Chapter Five</u> discusses the initial decision we must make in order to keep plowing in our role to advance God's Kingdom. We must begin by committing our life fully to God. If we are fully committed, we are more likely to keep moving forward in every circumstance.

In <u>Chapters Six through Thirteen</u>, we will look at five truths, laid out for us in Romans 8:18-39, designed to help us to keep moving forward.

<u>Chapter Six</u> discusses the glories of the eternity awaiting each believer. Looking to our future in Christ helps us to hang on during difficult times.

<u>Chapter Seven</u> shows us that the Holy Spirit and Jesus pray for us all the time, assisting us to live for Him and make it through difficulty.

<u>Chapters Eight and Nine</u> lay out some of the good outcomes that God brings from hard situations.

<u>Chapters Ten through Twelve</u> discuss seven key provisions that God has given us to help us as we seek to live for Him. These are especially helpful when the going gets tough.

In <u>Chapter Thirteen</u>, we will see that there is not a thing that can separate us from God's love and how we can have and intimate walk with Him.

My prayer is that as you read *Finishing Strong,* you will gain tools that will help you to be an overcomer who plays his or her role in advancing the Kingdom of God in this generation. I pray that you will serve Him throughout your entire life so that you will come to the end of your life, *Finishing Strong.*

John W. Shuey

Mechanicsburg, PA

All scriptures are taken from the NIV Translation, unless otherwise noted.

CHAPTER ONE

A Life Worth Living (at any cost)

Ramzi, who lives in the Middle East, had formerly been a sheikh. In 2011 he gave his life to Christ. At first, they made fun of him, but when he began to lead others to Christ, they beat him. When that did not deter him, they beat his son, Samee, and left him for dead. Later they surrounded his home and pelted it with stones, which escalated to bullets. Ramzi forgave the man who beat his son. In talking about his situation Ramzi said:

> The grace of God is so great in our lives. It is without boundaries. Everything that happened truly was hard, but we are not upset. We are happy because God has chosen us, so we have given our lives completely to Him. Before we were living in a life of darkness and a life of ignorance. After we came to faith in Christ, we experienced joy like we have never experienced before. We see something new every day.[i]

Ramzi's words resonate with millions of believers around the world, both those who are experiencing various kinds of suffering (such as sickness, poverty, and persecution), and those who are living a more comfortable life, (who would not trade the life they have in Jesus Christ for anything else that you could offer them). They would declare that the life Jesus offers is the best life that is possible.

The Perfect Life

In order to get a glimpse of the wonderful life Christ

offers, we must first get a glimpse of the life of darkness and ignorance that Ramzi talked about. When we see how dark the darkness is, we will see how bright the light of Christ is, just like we see the brilliance of a diamond which is highlighted when placed on a dark cloth.

Jesus offers us the best life possible. He placed the first humans, Adam and Eve, in the Garden of Eden where they experienced fellowship with God as He came to speak to them during the cool of the day (Genesis 3:8). This fellowship with God provided time for them to get to know Him and ask Him anything that would enable them to make right decisions. In their original state, they knew nothing of sin and had no shame (Gen. 2:25). They were surrounded by plant life that provided both beauty and nutrition. There were surrounded by birds in the air, fish in the water and other animals. It was the place where God ruled, and it was amazing! God told Adam and Eve that they were to *"Be fruitful and increase in number; fill the earth and subdue it"* (Gen. 1:28). Although God had apparently not made the entire earth like the Garden, He commissioned Adam and Eve and their descendants after them to subdue the earth. In doing this, they would bring the rest of the earth under God's control thus making it as wonderful as the original Garden. They had been commissioned to bring the rule of God to all the earth.

Everything was open to them except one tree in the middle of the Garden. This was a tree called the *"Tree of the Knowledge of Good and Evil"* (Gen. 2:17).

The Life of Darkness and Ignorance

God created an idyllic life for Adam and Eve and their descendants. Humans were created to enjoy God's presence and His blessings and engage in His purpose to bring the entire world under His control. We may wonder how things could have started so good and ended up with millions living in darkness and ignorance.

Because God created humans in His image (Gen. 1:26-27), they were designed with a free will. They could not be "in God's image" without free will. He wanted them to love and serve Him because they chose to do so. Without free-will, humans would have been mere robots.

One day the serpent, really the devil,[ii] came to Eve in the Garden and sought to get her to eat from the "tree of the knowledge of good and evil." He told Eve that God was holding out on them. The serpent told her that if they ate the fruit from this tree, which God told them not to eat, they would be able to determine good and evil without the help of God. She ate from the tree and gave some fruit to Adam. When they ate, everything changed. They immediately felt the shame of their disobedience and hid from God. They experienced consequences of their actions such as having difficulty in growing crops and difficulty in childbirth (see Genesis 3). Even creation changed.

Adam and Eve's sin also caused them to become separated from God (Romans 6:23). They could no longer benefit from His wisdom and instruction. Life headed south quite quickly. Without God's input, Adam and Eve's son, Cain, killed his brother Abel, evidently thinking that was the best way to solve a problem he was having (Genesis 4). As we continue in Genesis 4, we find that the humans did succeed in a number of things, like domesticating animals, developing agriculture, music, and manufacturing through the forging of tools. Humans seemed to be making great progress. But then we find another man, Lamech, committing murder. People were able to accomplish certain things, but they had no ability to change their character. Life for humans quickly spiraled out of control. Moses tells us,

> *The LORD saw how great man's wickedness on the earth had become, and that every inclination of the thoughts of his heart was only evil all the time.* (Gen 6:5)

Because things had gotten so out of hand, God destroyed everyone, except for Noah and His family. The sin of Adam and Eve negatively impacted the whole human race, causing the following:

- All humans were born with a sin nature, which Paul describes as spiritual death because separation from God is spiritual death (Romans 6:23 and 5:12).

- Because sin caused a separation from God, humans became dependent upon their own wisdom, causing a devastating impact, which is clearly seen as we examine the history of the world. In our own day, we see violence, rape, war, racism, misogyny and all manner of evils committed by persons against others who, in many cases, think they are working for their own good and the good of others.

- Fallen humans continue to sin. As individuals and societies continue to add sin upon sin, they make their personal life and culture worse, as they accumulate a bigger and bigger burden of guilt and shame. Eventually, the guilt and sin become very difficult or impossible to bear.

- Creation itself was actually impacted by the sin of Adam and Eve. (We will talk about the effect of the Fall on creation in a later chapter).

- In addition to the above, all those who die without a relationship with God will spend eternity separated from God in a place the Bible calls hell. (We will be judged after death. See Hebrews 9:27).

It is no wonder that Ramzi said that he lived a life of darkness and ignorance.

But Jesus

Thankfully, Ramzi said that he no longer lives in ignorance, but possesses a life of joy. How could his life have changed so drastically? The answer is Jesus.

God grieved over the condition of the world. He wanted every man, woman, boy, and girl to experience the fellowship with Himself that Adam and Eve had before succumbing to the temptations of the serpent. He wanted their lives to change. Being just, however, God could only forgive men and women of their sins if a just penalty was paid. The problem is, no human could pay for the sins of others because all humans have their own sin and guilt (Romans 3:23). The Israelites atoned for their sins by bringing sacrifices yearly, but the process had to be repeated every year which only reminded them of their sin (Hebrews 10:1-2). There was only one solution. God had to send His only Son to live a perfect life and sacrifice His own perfect life to pay the penalty for everyone:

> *For we do not have a high priest who is unable to sympathize with our weaknesses, but we have one who has been tempted in every way, just as we are--yet was without sin.* (Hebrews 4:15)

Jesus, the perfect man, died to pay the penalty for the sins of all of us!

> *For Christ died for sins once for all, the righteous for the unrighteous, to bring you to God.* (1 Peter 3:18)

There is much truth packed into this one verse. First of all, He paid the penalty for our sins. Those who have received Christ into their life are no longer guilty of sin. The penalty has been paid! Therefore, those who have received Him do not need to carry the burden of sin, nor do they need to walk in shame. They are like ex-cons who have not only been pardoned, but whose record has been expunged. There is no rap sheet. A thousand-pound weight has been lifted from their shoulders. They are free from their past indiscretions and can now move into a new life without the shadow of the past.

Secondly, we noticed that Jesus not only released us from

guilt and shame, but He also brought us to God. This means that we have the opportunity to get to know the greatest Person in the universe. I am writing this chapter on the 43rd anniversary of the day I asked my wife, Kerry, to marry me. We had only known each other for twenty-eight days, but we both felt led by the Lord to get married. I have spent the last 43 years getting to know the most amazing earthly person. After all these years, I am still amazed at the depth of character and love that I see in her. As wonderful as it has been to get to know Kerry, I have the opportunity to know Someone who is infinitely greater than her. Those who have received Christ are no longer separated from Him! We can get to know Him and be recipients of His wisdom and love.

As we interact with Him through reading His Word (the Bible) and praying, we not only get to know Him, but we begin to see how He wants us to live. This life He has planned for us is not at all like the life of darkness and ignorance that we lived before. Jesus said, *"I have come that they may have life, and have it to the full"* (John 10:10). This is the life of joy experienced by Ramzi and can be experienced by all who embrace Christ as Savior and Lord.

In addition, God makes Himself available to us. When we face situations where we need wisdom and strength, He welcomes us to come to Him.

If any of you lacks wisdom, he should ask God, who gives generously to all without finding fault, and it will be given to him. (James 1:5)

We may ask, "how can I live differently?" I remember how weak I used to be. Back then, all I could do was to seek Jesus to forgive me of my sins, but Jesus not only died to pay the penalty for our sins, He rose from the grave to make it possible for us to live a new life. Paul said, *"...Just as Christ was raised from the dead through the glory of the Father, we too may live a new life."* (Romans 6:4) When we asked Jesus to come into our life and to forgive our sins, the Bible tells us that we are *born again* or *born from above* (John 3:16). This happens when the Holy Spirit[iii] comes into our lives and connects us with God. He lives in us, helps us to overcome our past weaknesses, and live the life He always wanted us to live.

At the end of Romans 7, Paul tells us about the struggles he had when he tried to be obedient to God but couldn't. In frustration, he asks *"Who will deliver me from this body of death?"* He recognized that he could not do it on his own. He then tells his readers the answer that he discovered:

> *Therefore, there is now no condemnation for those who are in Christ Jesus, because through Christ Jesus the law of the Spirit of life set me free from the law of sin and death. For what the law was powerless to do in that it was weakened by the sinful nature, God did by sending his own Son in the likeness of sinful man to be a sin offering. And so he condemned sin in sinful man, in order that the righteous requirements of the law might be fully met in us, who do not live according to the sinful nature but according to the Spirit. (Rom 8:1-4)*

We have not only been forgiven of our sins, but because He sent the Holy Spirit has come to live in those who have received Jesus, we can begin to live the life that God desires, a life which expresses character qualities such as love, peace, joy, self-control and so on (Galatians 3:22-23). We can progressively become more and more like Jesus!

A Restored Purpose

God has not only restored us to a relationship with God where we can know Him and progressively become more and more like the Lord Jesus, He has also restored the purpose He gave to Adam and Eve. Before, Jesus went into heaven, He commissioned His disciples, telling them:

All authority in heaven and on earth has been given to me.

Therefore go and make disciples of all nations, baptizing them in the name of the Father and of the Son and of the Holy Spirit, and teaching them to obey everything I have commanded you. And surely I am with you always, to the very end of the age (Matthew 28:18-20).

Remember that at creation, God gave Adam and Eve and their descendants the responsibility to fill the earth and subdue it. In other words, He wanted them to take His Kingdom -rule to every part of the world. Because they sinned against God, they became separated from God and His wisdom. Instead of fulfilling their purpose, they failed miserably. God's purpose for humans upon earth seemed doomed.

Now Jesus says: "I have given you a life worth living! I have restored you to a relationship with God! I have given you a life where you know God personally; a life where you can win over temptation and do the right thing; a life where you can be more and more like Jesus and experience the peace and joy that only He can give; a life where you can live as My followers, or disciples."

Before He went back to heaven, Jesus told His followers that they should go to every nation (ethnic group)[iv] preaching the Gospel and teaching them to become His followers. In so doing, they will take His kingdom to the ends of the earth. The Church, His followers, have been doing this for nearly two thousand years. The result is that there are billions of believers around the world in thousands of ethnic groups. The progress has been encouraging, but there is much more to be done with thousands of ethnic groups still to be reached with the truth of Jesus' Gospel.

God changes our character, but He also supplies each individual believer with what they need to play their part in taking the Good News to those around us and those in other parts of the world. First of all, He has given each of us an individual purpose that enables us to have a significant role in taking the Good

News to the ethnic groups of the world:

For we are God's workmanship, created in Christ Jesus to do good works, which God prepared in advance for us to do. (Ephesians 2:10)

God designed each of us with a purpose before we were ever born. He designed us with the qualities that we would need to fulfill the purpose that He prepared for us. He took us from being weighed down and burdened by sin, where we failed to know Him or fulfill His purpose, to a life where we walk in fellowship with Him and we fulfill the purpose He prepared for us before creation ever took place.

We may ask how we can go from being a sinner to fulfilling the purpose of God. Once again, the answer is the ministry of the Holy Spirit. Jesus understood human weakness, even in His personal disciples whom He trained Himself. For this reason, He told them that they should not begin His Commission for them immediately, but they should wait to be empowered by His Spirit, saying,

But you will receive power when the Holy Spirit comes on you; and you will be my witnesses in Jerusalem, and in all Judea and Samaria, and to the ends of the earth (Acts 1:8).

On the Day of Pentecost, the Holy Spirit came upon them and gave them power and they accomplished much!

Not only has He created us with a purpose, but He has endowed each believer with supernatural abilities, called spiritual gifts, to assist us in fulfilling our God-ordained purpose (see Romans 12 and 1 Corinthians 12 to discover what some of these gifts are). [v]

The disciples waited and they received power and gifts for ministry. Over the past 2000 years, each successive generation of disciples has produced an ever- increasing number of disciples who have been accomplishing the purposes of God throughout the earth.

There's More

God also wants us to experience the wonder of His joy-filled life for us for all eternity. Although we will talk about the details of this life in a later chapter, I want to talk about our eternal life just a little to whet our appetite for all that God has for us. In eternity, we will take off our mortal body and have one that is incorruptible (1 Corinthians 15:42). In eternity, there will be no more death, mourning, crying or pain (Revelation 21:4), and we will be like Jesus (1 John 3:2). But even greater than all of these, we will live with the Lord forever (1 Thessalonians 4:17). Imagine living in the presence of this infinite God forever. What a great privilege.

God has provided an indescribable life for us. He has given us forgiveness of sin and a new life that includes a personal relationship with Him where we can walk in victory over sin, becoming more and more like Jesus, living a life that will last forever.

In addition, He commissioned us to play a part in helping to fulfill God's ultimate purpose to bring people from every ethnic group in the world to Him. I trust that each of you reading this book is saying, "I want live like that. I want to know Him! I want to fulfill my purpose! I will give everything that I can to do my part!"

There is, however, a price to be paid:

Jesus replied, "No one who puts his hand to the plow and looks back is fit for service in the kingdom of God." (Luke 9:62)

The fact that Jesus implies that there may be some who do not keep moving ahead indicates that not all believers fulfill their purpose. In the next chapter, we will be looking at some people who did not fulfill all that God had for them, and some of the reasons why. We will also meet people who went through horrible difficulties but *did* fulfill God's plan. Our purpose in this book is to help us to be like those who make it, in spite of difficulties and roadblocks. Let us move forward, determined that even if roadblocks come, we want to know Him and fulfill His purpose for our lives.

CHAPTER TWO
Being Faithful Has Its Challenges

My wife and I were conducting meetings with our good friend, Pastor Manish Pagare, in Nasik, Maharashtra, India. We had spent the morning talking about leadership in the church. As the day went on, we gave opportunities for the pastors to give testimonies. One pastor from outside the city got up and shared his story. A number of people had come to know Jesus through his ministry. They planned on having a large (for that area) baptismal service. Some radical Hindus found out about the meeting. After the meeting, they began to beat this pastor mercilessly. He was about to be killed when his wife realized that one of the men inflicting the beating was a relative and begged him to spare her husband's life. Because of the importance of family in Asia, they stopped the beating and the pastor lived. However, his near- death experience did not deter him from continuing to do the will of God in his life. He continued to move forward with God's plan for him.

As we meditate upon the wonders of the joy-filled, peace-filled, purpose-filled life we described in Chapter One, we might expect that every believer would do the same things as the pastor in Nasik. Indeed, many have been tempted and suffered for the cause of Christ over the last two thousand years and continued to fulfill His purpose for their lives in spite of their hardships. As a result, the Gospel has begun to take root in 10,000 of the nearly 17,000 ethnic groups in the world.[vi]

But, as we look at the Scriptures and church history, we

find that not everyone who began with Jesus kept plowing (see Luke 9:62 again). Some, after experiencing pain, hardship or suffering, surrendered to temptation, and others failed to complete the mission that God had laid out for them. In the next section of this chapter, we will focus on some individuals who started out serving the Lord but did not finish well. I mention these individuals as a warning to the reader, while highlighting some of the pitfalls that can trip believers up. The latter part of the chapter will highlight those who, in spite of severe struggles and tests, completed the task God had for them. We don't have space to include long portions of Scripture in the text of this book, so I have included an endnote for each of the people we talk about so you can see where their story is in the Bible, and read more. The remainder of the book will provide principles designed to help us overcome challenges and complete the work that God has called us to.

Servants Of God Who Did Not Finish Strong

Balaam [vii]

Israel had left Egypt heading toward the land that God had promised them. Balak, the king of Moab, noticed that the Israelites had easily defeated the Amorites and was not confident that he could defeat Israel. Therefore, he hired the prophet Balaam to curse Israel. Initially, God told Balaam not to go with the Moabites, but Moab kept approaching Balaam to come. God finally relented and allowed Balaam to go. Balaam made it clear to Balak that he would only declare what the LORD told him to say. His first declaration blessed Israel. Balak went to him again and again, optimistic that Balaam would speak a curse over Israel, but each time Balaam spoke he spoke a blessing from God over Israel, at one time saying:

> *God is not a man, that he should lie, nor a son of man, that he should change his mind. Does he speak and then not act? Does he promise and not fulfill?* (Numbers 23:19)

God made it clear that He was not going to change His mind concerning Israel. God had a role for Israel to play in advancing His Kingdom, and He would not relent. Both Balak and Balaam were sad; Balak because Israel had been blessed and Balaam because he was going to miss out on the prophet's fee.

However, Balaam had a sinister plan. He wanted the money even though it would mean he would miss out on fulfilling God's plan for His life and it would put Israel in jeopardy.

They have left the straight way and wandered off to follow the way of Balaam son of Beor, who loved the wages of wickedness. (2Peter 2:15)

Nevertheless, I have a few things against you: You have people there who hold to the teaching of Balaam, who taught Balak to entice the Israelites to sin by eating food sacrificed to idols and by committing sexual immorality. (Revelation 2:14)

The prophet's reward had been dangled in front of Balaam, but he could not collect it because God would not curse Israel, so Balaam devised a plan. He knew that the LORD could not bless Israel if she engaged in sin, so he told Balak to lure the Israelites to worship false gods and to engage in immorality. Balaam chose money over the will of God! Tragically, throughout history, some of God's people have chosen to pursue wealth, even though it meant missing out on God's best.

On one occasion, a young man[viii] came to Jesus to ask what he needed to do to inherit eternal life. Jesus told him to keep the Commandments. The young man said that he had kept all of them his entire life. Jesus then told him to give all his possessions to the poor, and he would have eternal life. The man went away without eternal life because he would not give up his riches to serve God.[ix]

Paul tells his disciple, Timothy, about a young man named Demas. He evidently showed great promise and became one of Paul's assistants, but, when Paul wrote about him to Timothy, he said:

> *"for Demas, because he loved this world, has deserted me and has gone to Thessalonica. Crescens has gone to Galatia, and Titus to Dalmatia.* (2 Timothy 4:10)

As Demas got a glimpse of what this world could provide for him compared to what he would receive in ministry, he decided that he would go after "this world" instead of serving the Lord with Paul, where he may have already experienced hardships and suffering. We don't know exactly what aspects of the world attracted Demas. It could have been pleasure, position in society, money, or all of the above. It likely did involve money. Jesus declared that you cannot serve both God and money (i.e., the one you serve is the one you look to in order to meet your needs) (Matthew 6:24). Although many wealthy believers down through the years have been used of God to fund the work of the Lord, *money can, and has been, a stumbling block to some.*

King Solomon[x]

King Solomon followed King David to the throne. He is considered the wisest man who ever lived, at least until the arrival of the Lord Jesus. Solomon possessed amazing wisdom. He demonstrated the mind of God in the way he led Israel. His wisdom was so great that when the Queen of Sheba came to visit him, she said that his wisdom and kingdom exceeded the report she had received (2 Chronicles 9:5-6).

Sadly, however, Solomon was led astray by his many idol-worshipping wives and concubines. God told Israel that she should only marry other Israelites. This was not because God was a racist, but because He knew that believers can be led astray when they marry non-believers. This is exactly what happened to Solomon. As his wives led him to sin, he led Israel astray (1 Kings 11:1-3). Solomon started well, but did not finish well. His love of women, and perhaps love of sex, led to his down fall.

I remember hearing a missionary, Don Young, speak in the late 1970's, not long after I became a pastor. He said the number one reason that a young person who is called to serve God in international ministry does not make it to the mission field is that they marry the wrong person. *Over the centuries many have failed to fulfill God's plan for their life because they have sought pleasure or failed to wait for the life partner of His choice.*

Ananias and Sapphira[xi]

By the time we meet Ananias and Sapphira, the Church has grown exponentially. Three thousand have embraced Christ as Lord following Peter's first sermon (Acts 2). As these believers formed into house churches, Luke, the writer of the Book of Acts, tells us that even more people received Christ. Over time, the Church discovered that some of their new brothers and sisters struggled financially. A man named Barnabas sold one of his properties and turned the proceeds over to the church leaders to assist the church to care for those less advantaged (Acts 4:34-37).

Ananias, and his wife Sapphira, decided that they too wanted to give some money to the poor. They also sold some property. When they brought the money to Peter, they told him that they sold the property for the amount they turned in. However, they had actually sold the property for more in order to keep some for themselves, but also look like they had sacrificed as much as Barnabas. In order to protect the integrity of the early Church, God struck down both Ananias and Sapphira. He did not strike them down because they only gave part of the money (See Acts 5:4), but rather because they lied.

As we saw in the case of Balaam, God blesses His people when they walk righteously. The leadership of the early church was also at stake. As you will see when you read the entire book of Acts, Barnabas played a large role in the spread of Christianity throughout the known world. Had Ananias and Sapphira's sin been left undetected, they may have become leaders in the Church. The fledgling Church could have been corrupted with leaders who did not have integrity. The Church is weakened when the wrong people become leaders. In fact, the entire Book of Jude warns believers to reject self-oriented leadership. *Some people fail to fulfill God's purpose for their lives because they seek a position in the Church that God did not intend for them, or they live for honor for themselves instead of seeking glory for God.*

Before I became a pastor, a young man who had some personal challenges (and was unqualified) desired a position in the church where I attended. He talked church people into voting him into office. The pastor was instructed by the Assistant District Superintendent to remove this person from office, so the pastor asked another elder and me to go with him. The man became so angry that he attacked the pastor (and could have been legally culpable). The pastor did not press charges. There were ministries this man could possibly have done, but his desire for honor, and sinful way of going about receiving it, could have shipwrecked him.

I have told you these stories because Paul tells us that we experience common temptations. As we seek to follow the Lord, we will be tempted with some of these same temptations. Let these stories serve as a warning to us to seek God for help in overcoming temptation when it comes.

Servants Who Were Tempted To Quit

In Chapter Three, we will discuss the fact that difficulties will come to us, even as believers. In this section we want to talk about some great believers who had accomplished great things for God, but almost quit because of difficulties.

Elijah[xii]

God called Elijah to prophesy in the northern ten tribes

of Israel after Israel divided. God sent him to minister to King Ahab, one of the wicked kings in Israel's history. Elijah had been used of God to perform many miracles. On one occasion, God told Elijah to prophesy that a drought would come. God brought a long drought which was designed to call the Ahab and the nation to repentance. Ahab did not repent. As a result, idolatry saturated the land.

Elijah decided that Israel needed to make up her mind whom she would serve. So he devised a plan, undoubtedly by God's direction, to call the false prophets together for a challenge. He told the prophets of the idols to build an altar and call on their god to supernaturally send fire and ignite the sacrifice. They did as Elijah had suggested. The prophets prayed for hours but nothing happened. Then Elijah built his altar and asked men to saturate it with water. He called out to God, who sent fire that consumed the water and the sacrifice. The false prophets were then put to death. Immediately after this, Elijah prayed, and it rained for the first time in three years (1 Kings 18:19-46).

Ahab's wife, Jezebel, became angry that Elijah had put an end to the worship of false gods, because it resulted in many people rejecting the false gods and embracing the God of the Bible. She told Elijah that she would kill him. Elijah feared for his life and said: *"I have had enough, LORD," he said. "Take my life; I am no better than my ancestors"* (1 Kings 19:4). Elijah felt alone. He said, *"I am the only one left, and now they are trying to kill me too"* (1 Kings 19:10). It did turn out that there were 7000 followers of the Lord that Elijah did not know about.

Elijah almost quit. He wanted to die. *We, too, can be tempted to slow down or quit when we are exhausted, which would seem to be why Elijah would back down to one woman, after defeating 850 prophets.* But Elijah did not quit. He had an encounter with God, recovered from depression and finished his race (see 1 Kings 19:11-17).

Elijah was not the only Old Testament prophet who wanted to quit. Jeremiah[xiii] had been called to preach to the Southern Kingdom of Israel, Judah. He prophesied during the reign of Josiah, the great reformer king who sparked revival in Israel. God, however, also commissioned him to preach when Israel lived in apostasy just prior to being destroyed by Babylon. Very few, if any, listened to hm. He wanted to quit. He accused the Lord of deceiving him, perhaps thinking that his preaching would bring about change. He cursed the day he was born (see Jeremiah 20:7-15).

I remember as a young man hearing teachers and preachers calling Jeremiah "the weeping prophet." In this case, he seems to have been depressed by the lack of results in his ministry, and by the fact that the whole nation seemed to be opposed to him. It would be enough to cause anyone to want to quit! But Jeremiah went on from there and finished the ministry which God called him to. A little later, Jeremiah prophesied:

> *This whole country will become a desolate wasteland, and these nations will serve the king of Babylon seventy years. "But when the seventy years are fulfilled, I will punish the king of Babylon and his nation, the land of the Babylonians, for their guilt," declares the LORD, "and will make it desolate forever.* (Jeremiah 25:11-12)

Seventy years later, Daniel, living in captivity, remembered this prophesy and began to pray that God would send Israel back to their land. Not long after that, Cyrus, King of the Medes and Persians, sent Jews back to the Promised Land to build the temple and eventually to restore the walls of Jerusalem. *Discouragement and depression can take the servants of God out. Jeremiah testifies that God's people can emerge from depression and continue to do the will of God.*

The Hebrews[xiv]

This group of believers started out very strong. Paul commended them for taking a stand in the midst of suffering, for enduring persecution and ridicule (and standing beside those treated that way), who sympathized with those in prison, and endured the confiscation of property (Hebrews 10:32-34). In other words, at one time they endured anything that came their way in order to remain faithful to the Lord. The fact that Paul had to remind them of this time indicates that they were no longer taking such a sacrificial stand for the Lord. It does not appear that they had left the faith, but they had cooled a bit. He is writing to stir up the passion that they once had so that they would finish the complete work that God had for them. His exhortation to them was: *But we are not of those who shrink back and are destroyed, but of those who believe and are saved* (Hebrews 10:39). In the remainder of the letter, he gives them teaching on what to do. We will talk about some of that teaching as we continue.

These Hebrew believers, at least for the time being, had cooled down somewhat. Frankly, we don't know what happened with them. We don't know if they repented and came back to a red hot commitment to the Lord. *Some people fail to keep plowing ahead to fulfill God's plan because they have been ridiculed, persecuted or suffered in some other way.*

Those Who Kept Going

The Scriptures also tell us about others who went through great difficulty and yet did not seem to waver.

Job[xv]

Job may be the most famous. He was a righteous man, who had a large family and great wealth. Early in the book, we find the angels presenting themselves to God. Satan was there and God asked if he had observed Job. Satan indicated that he believed Job had remained faithful to God because of the many blessings in his life. God said, "Let's find out." He allowed Satan to touch Job's family and possessions. He did. In one day, Satan killed Job's ten children and then destroyed all his livestock. We read:

> *At this, Job got up and tore his robe and shaved his head. Then he fell to the ground in worship and said: "Naked I came from my mother's womb, and naked I will depart. The LORD gave and the LORD has taken away; may the name of the LORD be praised"* (Job 1:20-21).

In the middle of unthinkable tragedy, Job worshipped.

Later, Satan came into God's presence again and complained that God had not let him touch Job. He indicated that if he could touch Job that Job would curse God. God allowed Satan to attack him physically but did not allow Satan to take his life. Satan inflicted painful sores upon Job. It was so bad that Job's wife told him to curse God and die.

> *He replied, 'You are talking like a foolish woman. Shall we accept good from God, and not trouble?' In all this, Job did not sin in what he said"* (Job 2:10).

In his personal pain, Job did not sin.

Because of Job's pitiful condition, some friends came to comfort him. They told him he was experiencing difficulty because there was sin in his life. Job maintained his integrity through it all. Now, I don't want to give the impression that Job did not need to grow. He did. At the end, God confronted Job, stimulating him to growth. However, he remained faithful to the end.

Although Job remained faithful, some do not remain faithful when suffering. Kerry and I were in the mall one day. We encountered a couple from the church. They told us that their daughter had been suffering from a very painful medical condition. The father told us that he was angry with God because He hadn't healed her. *Adverse circumstances can make or break us.*

Paul

Another person who suffered greatly in his life and in his service for the Lord is the Apostle Paul. Listen to his maladies:

Are they servants of Christ? (I am out of my mind to talk like this.) I am more. I have worked much harder, been in prison more frequently, been flogged more severely, and been exposed to death again and again. Five times I received from the Jews the forty lashes minus one. Three times I was beaten with rods, once I was stoned, three times I was shipwrecked, I spent a night and a day in the open sea, I have been constantly on the move. I have been in danger from rivers, in danger from bandits, in danger from my own countrymen, in danger from Gentiles; in danger in the city, in danger in the country, in danger at sea; and in danger from false brothers. I have labored and toiled and have often gone without sleep; I have known hunger and thirst and have often gone without food; I have been cold and naked. Besides everything else, I face daily the pressure of my concern for all the churches. (2Corinthians 11:23-28).

In addition to this, Paul[xvi] has at least one physical limitation. He went to the Lord three times asking Him for healing. Jesus told Paul that He would not heal him, but that His grace was enough (2 Corinthians 12:9). In spite of this, Paul ministered in at least thirteen cities and provinces, planting churches in many of them. In addition, he wrote many letters, some of which are part of the New Testament, to bring instruction, answer questions and bring correction where the churches were in error. It was this Paul who declared that he had finished the race to which God had called him.

Peter

The Apostle Peter[xvii] also completed his race, although he experienced great difficulty. Most readers would not have expected Peter to weather difficulties. On the night before Jesus would face His trial, He asked Peter and two others to pray with Him late at night. They fell asleep. Then, when Jesus told them that He would face a trial and execution, Peter vowed that he would not betray Jesus even if it meant that he would die with Him. Later, Peter denied that he knew Jesus three times.

Yet Jesus saw potential in Peter and chose him to be the leader of the early church. After the Holy Spirit came, Peter preached boldly. As the Church began to gain traction, Peter and John were pulled before the Jewish religious authorities and told not to preach any more about Jesus. Peter said, "We must." They left there and went out to preach. On another occasion, Peter was imprisoned and facing execution. He was rescued. Even after imprisonment, he continued in the work.

Tradition tells us that Peter eventually was crucified for preaching Christ. He felt unworthy to be crucified like Jesus, so he asked them to crucify him upside down.[xviii]

Down through the ages many dedicated Christians have faced great difficulty and persecution, but finished their race. Let me give you one example. There was a man from India who received Christ under most difficult circumstances. Those who opposed Christianity came to him to force him to recant his faith. He replied, "I have decided to follow Jesus." Archers killed his two sons when he refused. They threatened his wife and he said, "Though no one go with me, I will follow." They killed his wife. Then they took aim at him and he said, "The cross before me, the world behind me." You may wonder how we know this story. Well, when the villagers saw his commitment, they converted to Christ.[xix] Later, this story was turned into the song, "I Have Decided to Follow Jesus."

Believers continue to suffer in many ways and some face great persecution, and yet they remain faithful to the end.

It is important to understand that sometimes there is a time when you may need to slow down to deal with an issue in your life. When Nehemiah was told that the workers were going to be attacked, they carried tools in one hand and a sword in the other. This would slow them down. However, they had a situation that needed to be addressed, while continuing to work. (See Nehemiah 4). In the same way, someone may decide that they must put their regular routine on hold while they get some treatment.

Over 20 years ago my pastor, Dave Hess, found out that he had a very serious kind of cancer and that he would probably die. He wanted to continue to serve the Lord and did as much as he could from his hospital bed and recovering from home, but spent much time in the hospital receiving treatments. He took the time to get treatment, assisted by a series of amazing miracles, and is going strong today.[xx]

Others may need to set time aside to assist a child in need or to repair a damaged marriage. But, if my attitude is "I have this thing that needs corrected, but I am going to work on it with God's help and get right back to His plan for my life with whatever adjustments are necessary." I will be one who keeps my eye on the goal and keeps plowing. In addition, there may be times when the situation does not get corrected. It may be a non-life-threatening illness, like Paul's, or a relationship that doesn't seem to be able to be repaired, even though we have tried.

Believers down through the years have suffered many things which either got them sidetracked or could have. They have suffered physical afflictions, loss, persecution, imprisonment, beatings, temptations to materialism, immorality, and hunger for notoriety. They have suffered rejection and all manner of affliction. Some have quit their service to God, some became less passionate in their walk with God, and some kept going in spite of difficulties, finishing the race that God had for them.

If you are like me, you want to be the person who keeps

going without looking back. You want to be the one, who hears God say, "well done, good and faithful servant" at the end of life. You want your life to advance God's Kingdom and bring glory to His Name. In the next two chapters, we will continue to explore suffering and its causes, and then the remainder of the book will talk about all that God has provided to enable us to *Finish Strong.*

CHAPTER THREE
Suffering Happens

Author and Pastor David Platt tells about two teenage Chinese Christians, Shan and Ling. These teenage young men had been commissioned to take the Gospel where there is no church. Ling said, "I have told my family that I will likely never come back home. I am going to hard places to make the Gospel known, and it is possible that I will lose my life in the process." Shan added, "But our families understand. Our moms and dads have been in prison for their faith, and they have taught us that Jesus is worthy of all our devotion."[xxi]

Other Chinese believers express the same attitude. For several decades now, Chinese believers have had a heart to head toward Jerusalem and preach in all the countries between them and Jerusalem. Their goal is to send 200,000 missionaries, anticipating that 10,000 could be martyred.[xxii]

When many of us hear of the faith of Chinese believers, we may be awestruck by their commitment but conclude that God would never ask believers to pay such a price. We may feel that God may not even expect us to "keep plowing" (Luke 9:62) under many of the circumstances discussed in Chapter 2. I was discussing the issue of persecution and martyrdom one day. A friend responded with a question: "But those who are martyred are martyred because they've chosen to, aren't they?" Some preachers and teachers in our day indicate that believers should never experience the kinds of difficulties we have discussed previously.

So, who is right? Will Christians experience suffering, or should we expect that our faith will shield us from all suffering?

Looking To The Source

If you have made it to this point in *Finishing Strong*, you have noticed that I continually refer you to the Word of God, the Bible. I do this because the Bible is the only place that I am confident that I am getting 100 percent truth. As Jesus prayed for His disciples and those who would become disciples after them, He asked God to sanctify them (set them apart for service to God) in truth. He concludes that it is God's Word, the Bible, that is truth. *"Sanctify them by the truth; your word is truth"* (John 17:17). Great men and women of faith through the centuries have sought to know God and understand how to live by devouring God's Word. The Apostle Paul told his your protégé, Timothy:

> *"All Scripture is God-breathed and is useful for teaching, rebuking, correcting and training in righteousness, so that the man of God may be thoroughly equipped for every good work."* (2Timothy 3:16-17)

Paul assured Timothy that the Scriptures, the Bible, came directly from God. It provides the teaching that we need for life. It rebukes us when we get off course, corrects us so we can get back on the right track, teaches us how to walk the right way, and equips us to do good works. In other words, we need the Bible for every aspect of our lives. Jesus tells us that a man who does not make the Bible the foundation for his life is like someone who builds a house without a foundation that gets washed away by a severe storm:

> *'But everyone who hears these words of mine and does not put them into practice is like a foolish man who built his house on sand. The rain came down, the streams rose, and the winds blew and beat against that house, and it fell with a great*

crash." (Matthew 7:26-27)

Therefore, it stands to reason that if we want to get a definitive answer concerning whether Christians will experience suffering, we should look to the Bible.

A Sobering Discovery

As you can tell, I love the Bible and I love to study it. I enjoy the fact that studying the Bible is part of my "job," but, I don't just study the Bible to get sermons. In fact, I am often involved in a Bible Study not related to upcoming sermons. I am studying to learn, to grow in godliness, and to gain wisdom. Many of my sermons and seminars come from personal study.

Several years ago, I began a study of Romans chapter eight. The beginning of this chapter talks about the life that Jesus gives us when we both receive the Holy Spirit at salvation and continue to walk with Him. At the end of chapter seven, Paul discusses his own inability to do what he knows is right, decrying how easy it is to do what he knows is wrong. In frustration he asks, *"Who will deliver me from this body of death?"* (see Romans 7:14-25). In Chapter Eight, Paul answers his own question. He says the Holy Spirit enables us to live the life God wants us to live, the life we can't live by our own efforts.

As I continued my study, I came across a verse that hit me like a bucket of cold water.

"Now if we are children, then we are heirs--heirs of God and co-heirs with Christ, if indeed we share in his sufferings in order that we may also share in his glory." (Romans 8:17)

I really enjoyed the first part of this verse. First, we are children of God. We have been invited into His family. We have been made a part of His family to be loved like a son or daughter. God shows us that this adoption is legally binding when He tells us that we are his heirs, even co-heirs with Jesus. We inherit all the blessings and benefits that belong to Jesus! This means that we are recipients of His unconditional love and everything else we need, including eternity with Him. (We will talk about these in more detail in future chapters). I was excited to explore what it meant to be co-heirs with Christ. Then, I read the last half of the verse. We benefit from these blessings, **if** we share in His sufferings. It is **then** that we will share in His glory.

I had read this passage many times before, but this time the verse stopped me in my tracks like some kind of spiritual whiplash. Although this verse is important, I thought surely there aren't many corroborating verses. As I shared this verse with my wife, she reminded me of my seminary's class verse.

"I want to know Christ and the power of his resurrection and the fellowship of sharing in his sufferings, becoming like him in his death" (Philippians 3:10).

Once again, we resonate with the first part of the verse. As seminary students, we had given our lives to Jesus Christ. We had altered the course of our life in order to begin a career in ministry. We loved Christ and we are thankful for all He had done, and was continuing to do in our life. We wanted to know Him. Secondly, we wanted to experience the power of His resurrection. We wanted to live above the fleshly flaws that keep us from being more like the One that we love. Then we come to the last half of this verse. Perhaps when we have read this passage in the past, we have read "*I WANT TO KNOW CHRIST AND THE POWER OF HIS RESURRECTION and the fellowship of sharing in his sufferings, becoming like him in his death.*" In other words, did we read the first part of the verse with such excitement and fervor that we did not see the rest of the verse? Were we guilty of spiritual selective hearing?

We must get this. If we don't experience life, at least at some level, like He did, we won't truly get to know Him. Everything Christ did on earth, He did for us. He had died to His personal desires, except as they relate to what He could do for us. We will only know Him and His resurrection power as we die to ourselves and live our lives for Christ and for those to whom He sends us to care for. K.P. Yohannan, founder of Gospel for Asia says, "Here is one thing every follower of Christ must understand sooner or later: You cannot follow close to Jesus without suffering, no matter where you live in the world."[xxiii]

I came across another verse that is more shocking than the first two:

"For it has been granted to you on behalf of Christ not only to believe on him, but also to suffer for him," (Philippians 1:29).

The Philippians lived in poverty and persecution.[xxiv] The word translated "granted" in this passage comes from the group of words that give us the concept of grace. It carries with it the concept of favor or kindness.[xxv] We can all agree that God has graciously made it possible for us to believe in Him. John tells us that we cannot come to Christ unless we are drawn by Him (John 6:44). In other words, we will not seek God on our own, in a sinful state. The Holy Spirit works to show us the realities of the Gospel, helping us to recognize our need for Him, prompting us to reach out to Him for salvation. It is completely by grace. We don't deserve to know Him. Now we are told that we suffer by grace.

These are three clear verses indicating that suffering, on some level, is part of our walk in Christ. Since these verses were all written by Paul, albeit inspired by the Holy Spirit, we might say, "What did Jesus say about suffering?" While Jesus was spending His last night with His disciples, before the crucifixion, He said, *"In the world, you have trouble, but I have overcome the world"* (John 16:33). Although, we do see a ray of sunshine, Jesus says that we will have trouble in the world. As Jesus was preparing His disciples to take the Gospel to the world, He told them that it would not always be easy. Even though He is speaking a lot about persecution in John 15 and 16, I believe there is a broader principle here: Difficulty will come. Suffering Happens!

Does The Bulk Of The New Testament Agree With These Verses?

After I read Romans 8:17, I decided that I would see if this topic of suffering was prevalent in the New Testament, or if these were unique passages which may need to be interpreted based upon specific circumstances.   I began to look for words in the Greek that discussed some aspect of suffering. I found thirteen Greek words that described some type of suffering. These thirteen words were used 213 times in eighteen books of the New Testament. Of these 213 occurrences, over 130 talked about Christ's suffering and the suffering believers. The vast majority of these 130 verses discussed the suffering of believers. These thirteen words appear in eighteen of the New Testament books. In addition, the Book of Jude warns about false prophets and leaders that could dilute the work of the church.

Suffering is mentioned over 100 times by every New Testament writer in at least nineteen of the 27 books of the New Testament.   There is no way that we can ignore the topic of suffering when we discuss Christian living.

Great, you made my day! Why would you tell me this?

You may wonder why I would take the time to tell you these things. First of all, it is in the Bible. As a Christian leader and teacher, I must tell you what is contained in the Scriptures. However, more importantly, I want to tell you so that you are not shocked when everything doesn't work as smoothly as you would like. Kerry and I were talking with a woman one evening. She had lost her father a few years earlier and still grieved the painful death that he endured at the end of his life. We listened compassionately and later went on to quote Jesus when He said, *"In the world, you have trouble"* (John 16:33). She immediately quoted that last half of the verse: *"but I have overcome the world."* She seemed to believe that if Jesus had truly overcome the world, that life should not be so painful. Of course no one wants to experience suffering of any kind, let alone great suffering (I sure do not), but she had been led to believe that believers should not experience suffering. As a result, she was disillusioned with God. She said she still believed in Jesus, but her disappointment with God prompted her to stop going to church where she had attended for years, the church both her mom and dad attended. Some in our day teach that believers should always be healed and should all be wealthy. Indeed, God does heal, and He does meet our financial needs and perform many other miracles, but when the demands and expectations of some believers aren't met, they can become upset with and bitter toward God.

We must teach everything that the Scriptures teach. It teaches that suffering is part of life and part of the Christian walk. As we shall see, some suffering comes because we are Christians. If we are told that everything will always go perfect, we will be shocked when we experience a difficulty that is not resolved immediately. We may become disillusioned thinking that God has not been truthful.

Any good coach will challenge a team to do their best. He will tell them their potential, but he or she will also tell them that it is going to cost them something. The reason is that when the practices get difficult, the team will not be shocked. We must understand that we will only finish the race God has set before us if we can keep plowing when there is mud or dry ground. Because we are not shocked that we have experienced difficulty, we will do our best to keep moving forward.

Jesus warned the disciples that things would not always go easily. He told them:

Remember the words I spoke to you: 'No servant is greater than his master.' If they persecuted me, they will persecute you also. If they obeyed my teaching, they will obey yours also. They will treat you this way because of my name, for they do not know the One who sent me. (John 15:20-21)

I have told you this, so that when the time comes you will remember that I warned you. I did not tell you this at first because I was with you. (John 16:4)

Jesus knew that the disciples would face resistance and they would face hardship. He warned them so that when difficulty came, they would remember the difficulty He went through, and so that they would not be shocked when they, too, had difficulty. I share this as a warning to you and to me. If we are going to finish the task that Jesus gave us, we are going to face various types of hardships. Because we have been warned, we will more easily plow through difficulties the way Jesus did. In so doing, we will fulfill His plan for our life.

What Shape Does Our Suffering Take?

We may wonder what our suffering will look like. The truth is that it will look different for every person and family. Even when we face similar obstacles, we will experience them in different ways. As I looked at the meanings of the thirteen words that I used in my study, I found seven categories of suffering. (I know that there is an overlap, and we may experience more than one of these with the same event or circumstances.) I have not placed these in any kind of order.

Temptation

No temptation has seized you except what is common to man. And God is faithful; he will not let you be tempted beyond what you can bear. But when you are tempted, he will also provide a way out so that you can stand up under it. (1 Corinthians 10:13)

Paul tells the Corinthians that everyone experiences temptation. This temptation comes from multiple sources. Jesus told his disciples that some of those who follow Him will give into to temptation, but woe to the one who brings it (see Matthew 18:7). Some temptation comes from other people. This can particularly happen to Christians who seek to walk a righteous life. Other people that know them may feel that the person who is living righteously is missing out on what life is all about, or they may want to get them to join them so they can think they, themselves, are not so bad.

Others may fall into temptation because they give in to their own desires in areas where they have not yet gained victory in Jesus (James 1:14). Lastly, Satan and his emissaries tempt us (see Matthew 4:1-11).

Affliction /Hardships

"We are hard pressed on every side" (2 Corinthians 4:8). I have taken the idea of affliction from the word translated "hard pressed." It is similar to another Greek word meaning "hardships." As we continue to read this passage, we find that Paul includes many things such as being beaten, shipwrecked, perplexed, and left for dead. This word indicates the difficulties or sufferings that may come our way as a result of following the Lord. Stories are told of missionaries who would go to into foreign missionary service with their belongings in a casket, knowing they would never come to their homeland.[xxvi] Of course, many of these missionaries would face hostile people, disease, unfamiliar surroundings, or enduring the death of family members in their new country.

Hardships or afflictions can also include financial difficulties. Many pastors who lead medium to smaller churches, even in the U.S., may get smaller salaries than they would get in other careers. This can cause hardship for the families. This is multiplied in "Majority World" nations.[xxvii] In many cases, they receive no salary and must work in their fields and pastor at the same time. I remember speaking in a church in India. Pastor Manour and his family lived in an "apartment" attached to the church. I have no idea how he and his family lived in that small space. We sat on their beds in order to have tea. They cooked in that room and evidently had a small room or two behind this. They did this so that they could serve their community and preach the Gospel.

We have a very dear friend[xxviii] who grew up in a Christian home. His grandparents were the first to come to Christ in their village. They were kicked out of the village, and had to get their own water and food. This was a great cost. My friend, the grandson of this couple, wanted to become a doctor, but God called him to become a pastor, which he does quite well. Living on a pastor's salary in that part of the world, however, is quite different than living on a doctor's salary. He doesn't regret the decision, but it has caused many hardships for them.

I also want to talk about Jesus comment "In the world you have trouble" in this section. We need to understand that some affliction and hardship comes from living in this fallen, corrupt world. We will deal with this in greater detail in the next chapter, but I want to mention that there are hardships like sicknesses, natural disasters, and relational problems that have come about because we live in this fallen world. These can cause other problems such as the economic impact of a pandemic or natural disaster.

Testing

Blessed is the man who perseveres under trial, because when he has stood the test, he will receive the crown of life that God has promised to those who love him. (James 1:12)

I was receiving training from a ministry at The Pennsylvania State University. The trainees were helping to build a home for the directors of the ministry. I was taking up some grass so a walkway could be built between the sidewalk and curb. I was almost finished when the director asked me to move it. Thankfully, I responded appropriately and said, "I will move it anywhere you would like it." He didn't want me to move the walkway, but was just testing me to see if I had a servant's heart. God tests us as well. His desire is that we pass the test.

Peter also talks about tests. He says that the passing of such tests proves that our faith is genuine (1 Peter 1:7). Even though these may merely be tests, they can be quite painful. As Job pondered what he had experienced, he said, *"But he knows the way that I take; when he has tested me, I will come forth as gold* (Job 23:10).

It may be the "suffering" of needing to move a small walkway, or great suffering like Job experienced. Tests are not always easy.

Rejection

"Do not suppose that I have come to bring peace to the earth. I did not come to bring peace, but a sword. For I have come to turn "'a man against his father, a daughter against her mother, a daughter-in-law against her mother-in-law" (Matthew 10:34-35).

One form of suffering that many believers experience is rejection. New believers will often find that their friends no longer want to spend time with them after they begin to follow Christ because they can no longer engage in some of the activities that they once did, or because their friends don't like that want to tell them about Jesus. They reject the new Christian because they are rejecting Jesus.

Perhaps the most painful type of suffering a believer can experience is when members of their family reject them. Jesus said that it will happen. The reason is that when someone choses to become a follower of Jesus, they have a different philosophy of life. God is their master. They seek to do what He wants. If the family members do not know Him, they have different values, which can cause a rift between them.

In her book *Hiding in the Light,* Rifqa Bary tells of receiving Christ at age 12. Things were not too bad until she was baptized at age 16. Her family became incensed and her father told her that because she had converted from their religion and brought shame upon them, he would have to kill her.[xxix] The book outlines her incredible pain and God's marvelous intervention in her life.

Although, not on the same level as Rifqa's situation, we have discovered that many parents in the U.S. have experienced abandonment by their adult children. We continually become acquainted with Christian parents who are currently experiencing this tremendously painful phenomenon. Some even withhold their grandchildren from them. This is a form of suffer that is heartbreaking and on the rise.

Persecution

If we have read through the Bible, we do not get very far into the Gospels before we see Jesus being rejected because of His teaching. After He goes back to heaven, we see Peter and Paul placed into prison, Stephen and James executed for their faith, and the resistance from Jewish leaders and leaders of a variety of religions throughout the Roman Empire.

Persecution continues to occur at a record pace. In fact, more Christians were martyred in the 20th century than all other centuries combined.[xxx] I have a good friend who lost his mother and child in a bomb blast a number of years ago. The bomb had been detonated at a church because the bombers hated Christianity. Persecution causes pain and great suffering.

Being Weighed Down

As I mentioned above, Paul had many difficult experiences. He lays many of them out in his second letter to the Corinthians. At the end of the list, he says, *"Besides everything else, I face daily the pressure of my concern for all the churches"* (2 Corinthians 11:28). Paul had planted many of these churches and cared about others that he did not plant. He was concerned that they would grow and develop as the Lord desired, and he was often told about problems that existed in these churches. He carried a God-given burden for them. It weighed him down at times. I know a little of how that works. Twenty years ago, I served as pastor of a midsized church. I felt the burden for the spiritual care of the people and of seeking to develop a vision for the church at large. Even though I lead a small congregation, I experienced that weight of responsibility.

Paul also talks about the weight of living in this world, where we are less than perfect. Although we are growing in the grace of God, we still know that we carry attitudes and engage in actions that are less than perfect. As we seek to move ahead in our Christian growth, we sometimes groan to become more like Jesus (see 2 Corinthians 5:4).

Emotional Pain

Peter tells us that Satan prowls around like a roaring lion seeking someone to devour. The word used here to describe suffering carries with it the idea of emotional pain. Satan sometimes seeks to devour us by playing on our emotions. For instance, he may trick you into committing some sin by whispering in your ear that it is not so bad. ("God won't mind just this one time"). Once we have given in, he will then tell us that we are a failure and God could never forgive us for that. Or he may tell us that God can't use us now. It creates emotional anguish.

When there is a relational problem, he will haunt you with thoughts concerning what you have done wrong. Even if you did do something wrong, the Holy Spirit does not come in an accusatory way, but rather in a way that leads us to repentance, letting us know that we can do better. A couple of years ago, some people that my wife dearly loved sat her down and told her many things they thought were wrong with her, such as, "You are too friendly." Two years ago one of those individuals indicated that the relationship had come to an impasse and things would not continue as before. My wife was shocked and devastated. This happened in August, but my wife was an emotional wreck. She did not sleep well. We had a trip to Africa planned where we could share two weeks of teaching that would take place from 9 AM to 4 PM each day, including translation, and she needed to be preparing. The trip was in May, but she was not emotionally able to begin to prepare until March. (She did amazing, by the way, and learned much from the difficult experience.) Emotional suffering can be devastating.

Satan may tell a persecuted person, "You are alone. God does not care about you." We can also experience emotional pain when we lose a loved one or when we can no longer physically or mentally perform certain functions. The devil will seek to leverage these because he wants us to fall short of fulfilling God's plan for our life.

It is also important to note that emotional pain can come from all the above, including the pain that comes from the sicknesses, natural disasters, and relational problems that come from the Fall.

In Summary

I believe that we have seen that the New Testament talks a great deal about suffering. The Holy Spirit has not included this teaching to discourage us but to keep us from being shocked when it happens. He wants us to understand that both He and all believers down through the ages have suffered in one way or another. He also wants us to know that we can complete our race in spite of difficulty. But, we won't plow through difficulty if we don't understand that we may go through difficulty as we pursue our race with God. John Piper says, ""Wimpy worldviews make wimpy Christians. And wimpy Christians won't survive the days ahead."[xxxi]

The three passages that we began the chapter with not only tell us that we will suffer, but they also give us great promises. In Romans 8:17, we are told that we are joint heirs with

Christ, which means that as we go through the suffering we can look forward to eternity with God and the availability of all the resources to assist us in living for Christ now.

In Philippians 3:10, we find that we will truly get to know Christ as we share in His sufferings. This is the greatest gift we can receive. The context of Philippians 1:29, tells us that when we stand strong in the face of opposition, it exposes that the ones persecuting us are the ones who are defeated. In other words, they could not stop us. If they cannot stop us they cannot keep us from fulfilling God's will in our life.

We will finish our first section in the next chapter where we will explore the sources of suffering. After we have finished this first section which explains that suffering is part of life, what suffering looks like, and where it comes from, we will get to the meat of the book, and discuss what we can do to continue to accomplish the will of God, in spite of our suffering. In other words, how can we "keep plowing" when life happens and *Finish Strong*?

CHAPTER FOUR
What is the Source of Suffering and Evil?

I have extra time to study and write because we have been given a stay-at-home order from our President and Governor and a May discipleship trip to Cote d'Ivoire, West Africa has been postponed for one year due to the Covid-19 pandemic. The pandemic has caused leaders around the world to limit movement in order to slow down the spread of the disease, which as of today has killed around 105,000 people in the United States alone. We have been asked to limit our local travels to that which is essential, and many world leaders have limited travel between countries, which is why we will not go to Africa until next year.

Doctors and medical researchers have not yet developed treatments for Covid-19, in part because they do not know its origin. They believe if they knew the origin, they would have greater success in developing treatments.

In the same way, knowing the origin of suffering and evil will assist us in knowing which of God's remedies (provisions) to apply to our particular situation. However, it seems that most people are as perplexed about the origin of evil and suffering as the medical researchers are about the origins of Covid-19. A Barna poll asked responders if they could ask God one question, what would it be? The most common response was "Why is there so much suffering in the world?"[xxxii] In this chapter, we will discuss the origins of evil and suffering. Then, the rest of the book will be devoted to how to walk through suffering while continuing to do the will of God.

I want to encourage you to keep plowing through the first part of the book. It is important to talk about the fact that suffering is common to all of us, and to seek to have a basic understanding of suffering so that, with God's help, we can stand up under it, and *"after you have done everything, to stand"* (Ephesians 6:13). In the last two-thirds of the book, we will go into more detail about what God has provided for us, and how to access it so that we can walk through adversity victoriously.

THE FALL BEFORE THE FALL: The Original Source of Evil

In Chapter One, we began to talk about what theologians call the Fall. The Fall occurred when Adam and Eve disobeyed God, resulting in a number of changes to God's creative order that negatively impacted humans and our world. We briefly mentioned several of these in Chapter One. Let me list them again. We will explore these in great detail in this chapter.

We mentioned the following in Chapter One of this book:

- All humans were born with a sin nature, which Paul describes as "spiritual death," because separation from God is spiritual death (Romans 5:12 and 6:23).

- Because sin caused a separation from God, humans became dependent upon their own wisdom which had a devastating impact. This is illustrated throughout the history of the world. In our own day, we see violence, rape, war, racism, misogyny, and all manner of evils committed by persons against one another, who, in many cases, think they are working for their own good and the good of others.

- Fallen humans continue to sin. As individuals and societies continue to add sin upon sin, they make things worse and worse in the culture and accumulate a bigger and bigger burden of guilt and shame. Eventually, the guilt and sin become very difficult, or impossible, to bear.

- Creation itself was actually impacted by the sin of Adam and Eve. (We will talk about the effect of the Fall on creation in a later chapter.)

- In addition to the above, all those who die without a relationship with God will spend eternity separated from God in a place the Bible calls hell. (We will be judged after death. See Hebrews 9:27)[xxxiii]

A Fall occurred before the Fall in Genesis Chapter 3, however. It happened prior to the creation of Adam and Eve. At that time, God existed in heaven surrounded by a host of heavenly beings. The story of the Fall before the Fall is told by both Isaiah (Isaiah 14:12-17) and Ezekiel (Ezekiel 28:11-19).[xxxiv] It seems that one of the heavenly beings, called the Morning Star (Isaiah 14:12 -- some get the name Lucifer from this passage), was not satisfied with his place in the heavenly hierarchy because he was impressive. Ezekiel tells us that he was *the model of perfection, full of wisdom and perfect in beauty*" (Ezekiel 28:12). He was adorned with precious stones in mountings of gold, an anointed cherub. He was an awesome being. However, Ezekiel tells us that he became proud. Isaiah fills in a little more detail here. He reveals to us his heart:

> *"You said in your heart, 'I will ascend to heaven; I will raise my throne above the stars of God; I will sit enthroned on the mount of assembly, on the utmost heights of the sacred mountain. I will ascend above the tops of the clouds; I will make myself like the Most High'"* (Isaiah 14:13-14).

It seems that the Morning Star, Lucifer, was not content to play the significant role that God had given to him but wanted to make himself like the Most High. He wanted to be like God.[xxxv] God punished him by casting him out of heaven to the earth.

This seems to be the beginning of the Satan's war with God and is a precursor to Satan's temptation of Adam and Eve and the Fall.

The Impact Of The Fall On Humans And On Creation

God decided that He would establish His Kingdom on earth through humans. When Satan discovered that God wanted to work in humans and glorify Himself through them, he decided that he would do all he could to hinder God's plan. We have already discussed how the Fall happened on earth, in Chapter One. In this chapter, we will discuss the impact of the Fall. As we talk about the impact of the change in human nature and human culture, we must keep in mind that Satan lurks behind the whole process. He takes advantage of these changes to bring the greatest amount of devastation that he can.

We must also remember that Satan's temptation proved effective because Eve, and later Adam, had a desire to "play God" and determine what is right and what is wrong without the help of God. Adam and Eve's disobedience to God set in motion the problems mentioned above.

The Impact Upon Human Culture:

There have been many times in my life when I needed someone to guide me as I made a decision. I am grateful for those who have been mentors to me in ministry, Rev. Reynolds Waltimyer, Dr. Randall Corbin and Rev. Steve Hammer among many others. All of these men had served in pastoral ministry longer than I had and possessed great wisdom. I am sure they kept me from making a number of poor decisions that could have hurt me, my family and the congregations where I served. Think about people in your own life who have been there to give guidance when you didn't know what to do next. What might have happened if those people had not been there to guide you?

Adam and Eve had a much bigger problem. They had

been designed to walk with God. We know this is true because we see God seeking them out in the cool of the day (Genesis 3:8). But when they sinned against God by disobeying His direct command, their relationship with God was severed, leaving them to determine what was right and wrong on their own. Humans had been created to walk with God and hear His wisdom. After the Fall, they could no longer hear His voice.

Before, we begin to discuss the personal and cultural consequences of choosing to disobey God, we must briefly discuss why God would give humans the ability to choose, since He knew that things could go terribly wrong when they made wrong choices. Author Randy Alcorn, suggests that God gave man the ability to choose because free will it is part of bearing the image of God (Genesis 1:27. 5:1). He says:

> God is intelligent, creative, communicative, and free to choose. To be made in his likeness likely includes having these attributes, though on a finite level. We think because he thinks, we speak because he speaks, we create because he creates, and we choose because he chooses. These things all come from God and comprise part of what it means to be human.[xxxvi]

This power to choose not only includes our ability to disobey God, but also the power to choose to love or reject God. Had God made us with no choice, we would have been robots whose love for and obedience to God did not come because we chose to, but because we had been programmed to do so. Could we call that true love and obedience? I know my wife loves me. She tells me often and shows it often by the way that she treats me. Her love is obvious. I am amazed by the quality of her love and by the fact that she chooses to love me. I do not always know why she loves me, but it is great to be on the receiving end of it.

The Bible tells us that we love because He first loved us (1 John 4:19). The reason is that we would not know how to love if He had not first loved us. We still have a choice, however, if we want to return that love. I am sure that He enjoys the fact that we have chosen to love Him (with the Holy Spirit's assistance) as I enjoy being loved by Kerry.

I Can Bring Evil and Suffering Upon Myself

I was in the alley behind our back yard when I was a boy. I had gotten into a fight with my neighbor. We were rolling around on the ground and I was winning (not usual for me). About that time, my dad pulled up beside us to pull our family car into the garage. He merely said, "If you want to fight go in the yard." Notice, he was not breaking up the fight. He wanted us to do it somewhere where we would not be hit by a car. Then it happened. I looked up at him and stupidly said, "We will fight where we want to fight!" The fight with my neighbor ended as a new fight began! I immediately began to run to my bedroom (duh!). I opened the gate and shut it. Dad came over the gate and followed me to be room for some necessary discipline. I experienced some suffering that day because I made a very stupid decision!

My sin that day did not have major consequences and I learned an important lesson. However, we are all aware of people who have made tragic decisions. They make these decisions without the wisdom of God, which can bring serious life-long or eternal consequences.

Adam and Eve had two sons, Cain and Abel. When these two young men brought sacrifices to God, God accepted Abel's sacrifice, but Cain did not bring the kind of sacrifice God had asked for. God gave him a chance to bring an appropriate sacrifice but instead, he decided that the best course of action would be to kill Abel, perhaps thinking that if the "competition" were removed, he would be more acceptable. He made the wrong decision and God told him, *"When you work the ground, it will no longer yield its crops for you. You will be a restless wanderer on the earth"* (see Genesis 4:1-12). Cain brought this upon himself.

Jonah was an Old Testament evangelist who was called upon to call the archenemy of Israel, Assyria, to repentance. Jonah refused to do so and went in the opposite direction as fast as he could. He wound up in a terrible storm and in the belly of a large fish for three days.[xxxvii] This could not have been pleasant, but Jonah's hatred for Assyria caused his suffering.

We could possibly all cite people who destroyed their families through an affair or drug abuse. Others have caused psychological and physical damage upon themselves by having an abortion, or by losing a job because of laziness, or who faced jail time because they could not keep their anger in check. Sometimes we bring suffering upon ourselves by our own choices.

Our choice to reject God's offer of salvation has eternal consequences. Every one of us has sinned in many ways, coming short of God's desire for us (Romans 3:23). We have sinned in word, deed and thought more times than we can possibly count. We are all guilty before God, and we will all someday stand in judgment before God (Hebrews 9:27). We deserve to be eternally separated from God in hell. (See Revelation 20:12-15). But this does not have to be our fate. God has provided a way to change the direction of our life through the death and resurrection of Jesus. We can be forgiven for our sins. We can be forgiven by recognizing that Jesus has provided forgiveness for us by dying to pay the penalty for our sins. When we recognize that, we can come into a relationship with God by asking Him to forgive us of our sins, by asking Him to come into our life and by giving our life completely to Him so that He can become our master, Lord. When we do this, our life will begin to take a new direction and we can begin to make choices with the aid of His wisdom. In addition, we will be headed to an eternity in the presence of God.

If you have never asked Jesus Christ into your life as Savior and Lord, sincerely pray this prayer:

"Lord Jesus, I confess to You that I am a sinner. I thank You that you died to pay the penalty for my sin. I ask You to forgive me of my sins and come into my life. Thank You for being my Savior. I now want You to be Lord of my life."[xxxviii]

We Bring Evil and Suffering Upon Ourselves Because of the Cultures We Create

As we have already seen, individuals make decisions that negatively impact their lives. Sometimes they make these decisions because they are rebelling, but many times they make these decisions because they are cut off from God's input. This can be devastating.

However, we rarely make decisions in a vacuum. We are social beings. Since we have lost access to the voice of God, we consult with each other. When we do consult each other, we have a group of people who are making decisions with little input from God. As these groups make decisions, they develop customs which are adopted by the group, often pushed by stronger members of the society. Peer pressure motivates people to comply with the customs. They are also passed down to their children. In the Old Testament, we find a group of people from the plane of Shinar who convinced each other that they should build a city for themselves, so they didn't need to obey God's command to go throughout the earth. In this case, they began living in rebellion to God. If left unchecked, their children would have learned each of the group decisions and lived in a similar fashion, but chose to punish them by confusing their languages at that point, causing them to move throughout the earth (see Genesis 11).

Although we will talk of the role of Satan a little later in the chapter, I must mention at this point that Satan does interject himself into the pool of ideas that humans utilize in their groupthink. When Satan's ideas are embraced, the decisions will not be good for people because they will be drifting further from God and engaging in activities that are not good for them. Often then, culture develops without God's input and adapts to Satan's.

This does not mean that these societies are all bad. Kerry and I have had the privilege of visiting Africa, Israel, India, Pakistan, Europe, and a few other countries. We have seen some beautiful things in all of these places. We love the respect that people in India have for those who are older. We should all learn that respect. The art and architecture in various parts of the world is unique and beautiful. We have some beautiful wall hangings and table runners from Pakistan, and artifacts from Africa, in our home which remind us of the talent and creativity of different cultures.

Generally speaking, the basic mores in these cultures take people away from the living God. Millions worship gods that are not God, which isolate them from the One True God. In addition, many secular philosophies that have steered people away from God enticed them to engage in immorality, to give their lives to money and power, and to model racist, misogynist, and xenophobic attitudes that have enslaved some and destroyed the esteem and opportunities of others. Tragically, the people trapped in many of these false religions, atheistic philosophies, and demeaning attitudes do not know that they are doing wrong because these attitudes are engrained in their culture. Because people have become convinced that their religions or philosophies describe the essence of life, they reject Christianity and persecute those who know the true God through rejection, beatings, imprisonment, and even murder. Cole Richards, president of Voice of the Martyrs says, "Christ taught that our labors would be carried out in a spiritual warzone - A world in which we are hated aliens, and stranger pursued by an enemy that would 'only to steal and kill and destroy.'"[xxxix] We should not be surprised when the prevailing cultures in our world oppose our life-giving message, but, by God's grace, we should seek to be undeterred.

Creation Has Been Corrupted, Which Also Brings Suffering

Our environment can cause suffering, some of it because we have made bad choices. We have started forest fires and caused pollution. These choices have destroyed people's homes and livelihoods and contaminated drinking water in parts of the world. This is part of the suffering that we have caused ourselves.

Something, however, happened to creation itself at the Fall. Paul tells us:

> *For the creation was subjected to frustration, not by its own choice, but by the will of the one who subjected it, in hope that the creation itself will be liberated from its bondage to decay and brought into the glorious freedom of the children of God* (Romans 8:20-21).

Since the Fall, creation has been in bondage, or slavery to decay. Therefore, our very planet is suffering decline, which may be responsible for natural poisons, natural disease, predatory animals and a host of other evils emanating from nature.

We see some of this immediately after Adam and Eve sinned. God told Adam that he would till the land by the sweat of the brow as he dealt with thorns and thistles, and Eve was told that she would have pain in childbirth. This may, be the reason for many of the environmental issues that we have discovered in recent days.

Satan Seeks to Cause Suffering Through Evil

We have already seen some of the impact of Satan on our world when he lured Adam and Eve into sinning against God, by influencing unregenerate men and women to develop cultures whose underlying philosophies and religions oppose God.

Unfortunately, this means that every generation of humans has experienced its share of suffering, because Satan continues to blind the eyes of those who do not believe in God. One reason that humans continue to make mistakes is that the god of this world has blinded the eyes of those who do not believe (see 2 Corinthians 4:4).

When I first became a believer, I couldn't understand why everyone didn't come to Jesus when we shared the Good News with them. My eyes had been opened and it seemed quite illogical to reject Christ. However, many did. The reason is that Satan had blinded people's eyes by hiding the benefits of following Jesus and making some other course of action seem more prudent. Satan works tirelessly to keep those who have not believed in Jesus in the dark concerning the amazing life that He provides for those who receive Him and follow Him.

Many of those with blinded eyes reject Christ and pursue a course of action that eventually takes them further down the road of darkness and ignorance. They may embrace a religion or philosophy of life that doesn't lead them to the truth of Jesus Christ, and instead pursue a hedonistic or immoral lifestyle. As people become entrenched in those lifestyles, they slip deeper into darkness, sometimes thinking they are enlightened. They become so convinced that they are living the right way, that they become tools in Satan's hands by convincing others to live like them.

Satan, however, doesn't stop seeking to blind eyes when a person becomes a Christian. He continues to try to keep believers from being all that God desires for them. Peter tells us: *Be self-controlled and alert. Your enemy the devil prowls around like a roaring lion looking for someone to devour* (1 Peter 5:8). In this next section, we will discuss some of the ways that Satan seeks to defeat Christians, or at least keep them from fulfilling God's full purpose for their life.

Satan Seeks To Keep Believers From Knowing

Everything That God Has Provided For Them In Christ.

*I keep asking that the God of our Lord Jesus Christ, the glorious Father, may give you the Spirit **of** wisdom and revelation, so that you may know him better. I pray also that the eyes of your heart may be enlightened ..."* (Ephesians 1:17-18).

Paul prayed that they would have a Spirit of revelation and that their heart may be enlightened. The fact that they needed to be enlightened indicates that they may have missed some very important truths that would assist them as they sought to do the will of God. If Satan can blind us to parts of our benefit package as Christians, we will fail to cash in on it. I remember a time early in my walk with God. I knew that I had received Jesus into my life, but couldn't believe anything as good as heaven could happen in my life. As I prayed and meditated on God's Word, He confirmed in my heart that as a believer, I would someday be with Him. Had I not gotten a personal revelation of this truth, Satan may have tripped me up and kept me from pursuing the destiny that God had for my life.

Let me say once again, this is why we must get a steady diet from the Word of God. As much as possible, we should spend time in God's Word every day. As we read, we should ask God to teach us truth and speak to us in our life situation and ministry. He will be faithful to do   so. As we read, we may discover some areas that we want to study in more detail. There are lots of Bible Study helps.[xl] Continually seek to get to know God better in the Word and learn about the many benefits He has given us in Jesus Christ.

Satan Participates In Causing All The Kinds Of Pain We Talked Of In Chapter Three.

We will not take space to go over them again. But when we suffer affliction or hardship or testing or persecution or sickness, we might become discouraged and quit. Satan does this work because He wants us to quit.

Satan is not alone.

Satan has an army of underlings that assist him in his evil work. Paul tells us:

> *"For our struggle is not against flesh and blood, but against the rulers, against the authorities, against the powers of this dark world and against the spiritual forces of evil in the heavenly realms" (Ephesians 6:12). He has this methodical army that seeks to hinder God's work to take* the Gospel throughout the earth and bring the world under God's control.

The ultimate source of our suffering comes from Satan as he rebelled against God prior to the Garden of Eden. He then caused Adam and Eve to sin, setting in motion a series of events that have created more suffering through our own decisions or following a godless culture. We suffer from disease and natural disasters because of the decay that is taking place in the world.

But we don't want to end on a negative note! Yes, we have suffering in this world, but Jesus said, *"I have overcome the world"* (John 16:33). We suffer at times because of the poor choices that we have made, but Jesus came to give us a new life where we are forgiven of our past, delivered from our shame and given the potential to live differently because the Holy Spirit has come to live in us when we received Jesus Christ.

> *"Therefore, there is now no condemnation for those who are in Christ Jesus, because through Christ Jesus the law of the Spirit of life set me free from the law of sin and death. For what the law was powerless to do in that it was weakened by the sinful nature, God did by sending his own Son in the likeness of sinful man to be a sin offering. And so he condemned sin in sinful man, in order that the righteous requirements of the law might be fully met in us, who do not live according to the sinful nature but according to the Spirit." (Romans 8:1-4)*

Yes, we experience suffering while we are living in this world, however Jesus came to give us a life that is full (John 10:10); a life filled with peace and joy; a life filled with purpose; a life that glorifies God! In the remainder of the book, we will see many things that God has provided for us so that we can live that full and joyful life, in spite of circumstances; a life that has an eternal impact; a life that will receive a "well done" from God when we go to be with Him!

CHAPTER FIVE
Starting Right:
(A Brief Introduction To Section Two)

In this section, we will talk about many benefits God has provided for us so that we might keep plowing ahead in our pursuit of God, finishing strong! He promised us that we would benefit from the full inheritance of Jesus if we suffer with Him (Romans 8:17). The remainder of Romans 8 (verses 18-39) gives us five keys to enable us to face difficulty and keep moving forward as we seek to fulfill the destiny God designed for us. However, before we get into these five keys, I want to briefly discuss the necessary starting point for our journey, if we are going to *start right*.

At the beginning of the book, we met Ramzi a man who gladly endured severe hardships to follow the Lord Jesus Christ, because of the joy he had found in Him. As we explored what it was about life in Christ that enabled Ramzi to walk in joy, we discovered the many facets of the glorious salvation that God has offered to us in Christ Jesus. All who have received Christ by faith, have been forgiven of all their sins and given a relationship with God. They have been indwelt by the Holy Spirit enabling them to become increasingly like Jesus Christ, walking in love, faith and peace, and to empower them to minister for Him. In addition, they have been guaranteed a place in a perfect heaven to be with God for eternity.

This is what salvation is all about. God wants everyone to live in the fullness of this salvation. Life in Christ is not a smorgasbord where we pick and choose the aspects of Christianity that we choose to put on our plate. I remember early in my Christian life when we shared the Gospel, we encouraged people to ask Jesus into their heart so they would go to heaven some day. Of course, those who receive Christ will go to heaven someday, but many people "prayed the prayer," assuming they could live the way they wanted, or at least decide the ways they wanted to obey God, before they would eventually go to heaven. It was merely an eternal life insurance policy. Others taught that you could receive Christ as Savior from sin and chose to make Him Lord of your life at some later date, if you chose to do so.

When we do that, we are still in control. The reason we come to Christ is because we have sinned against Almighty God, and our life is far short of the purpose for which we are created. In other words, I have sin in my life, I am separated from God and I need someone else to run my life. In addition, we come to understand that we have a God-given purpose in our life that we cannot fulfill without being connected to Him. I can only live in peace and joy if He is in charge. He is God and I am not! We are saved to become like Him and serve Him.

For some, this might sound new, so we will do what we always do when we want to understand God's truth. We will look to the Scriptures. Let's look at how Jesus recruited men to follow Him:

As Jesus was walking beside the Sea of Galilee, he saw two brothers, Simon called Peter and his brother Andrew. They were casting a net into the lake, for they were fishermen. 'Come, follow me,' Jesus said, 'and I will make you fishers of men.' At once they left their nets and followed him. (Matthew 4:18-20).

Jesus did not say, "Ask me to forgive your sins and someday you will go to heaven." He asked them to follow Him. They left their nets, their livelihood, and followed Him. Adam Clarke, a well-known Bible commentator in the 18th and early

19th Centuries, says "follow" means, "Receive my doctrines, imitate me in my conduct - in every respect be my disciples."[xli] Later Jesus asked twelve of His disciples to follow Him in the first century rabbinical sense. Lois Tverberg tells us what it meant to study under a rabbi:

> Often disciples would travel together with a rabbi, and they would take weeks away to go on a teaching trip. A disciple had to ask his wife's permission to be away from home to study longer than 30 days. When they traveled, rabbis and disciples would pool their money to buy food, etc. Jesus received contributions from wealthy women, and they were known for supporting other rabbis too. When they traveled, the villages they taught in were expected to extend hospitality, giving them food and shelter. [xlii]

This is what Jesus asks of us. He did not go through the rejection of humans, His creation, and the horrors of the cross in order for people to follow Him when it suits them. He wanted those who would pay any price to experience the fullness of the life He offered. He wanted them to go after it all.

Living this kind of life comes at a price. Most things that are worthwhile do. I enjoy hearing about the athletes who participate in the Olympics. We hear stories of those who get up early in the morning, go to work at their job and train some more after work. They are on a very strict regimen of workouts and nutrition. They do this for many years with the goal to make the team or, if they are fortunate, to get on the podium in their chosen sport. Paul discusses the ancient Olympics as he talks about his own commitment to following the Lord.

> *"Everyone who competes in the games goes into strict training. They do it to get a crown that will not last; but we do it to get a crown that will last forever. Therefore I do not run like a **man** running aimlessly; I do not fight like a man beating the air. No, I beat my body and make it my slave so that after I have preached*

to others, I myself will not be disqualified for the prize." (1 Corinthians 9:25-27)

He says athletes give themselves to training to win a wreath (or in the case of modern Olympics a medal), which is perishable, but we live a disciplined life to gain an eternal reward. We are doing it to finish the race God has laid out for us (2 Timothy 4:8), and to hear God say, "Well done." (Matthew 25:14-30). Should we not be willing to pay a greater price than Olympic athletes? Should we not be willing to be disciplined for Him? Should we not be willing to plow through hardships and persecution because of the glory that waits us on the other end?

Jesus said to His disciples (including disciples down through the ages):

"If anyone would come after me, he must deny himself and take up his cross daily and follow me. For whoever wants to save his life will lose it, but whoever loses his life for me will save it." (Luke 9:23-24)

He declares that He has life for us, abundant life, a life that is full (John 10:10). The life Jesus describes here is the Greek word *"zoe." Zoe* is the life of God. The abundant life that God gives to us is the very life of God living in us. It is the life of full salvation, culminating in an eternity with God in complete perfection. The life Jesus asks us to give up is the Greek word *"psyche."* It is the life we can produce on our own. Do we want the life God offers? Then we must take up our cross and follow Him. The cross came to Jesus because He followed God unreservedly. He has asked us to take up our cross. He is asking us to endure what comes our way as we follow Him unreservedly. It may be hardship that comes from living in the world or because we have obeyed Him. There may be things we must leave behind to follow Him. He may ask us to go to dangerous places.

The weekend before we left the U.S. for our first trip to Pakistan, a major magazine declared that Pakistan was the most dangerous place in the world. We went (my wife in faith, me in faith-but-trepidation), and God moved powerfully. God may ask us to go to dangerous places around the world or in our city. We may be rejected, even by members of our own family. Jesus says that if you do that, "*I will give you My Life!*" I will give you life to the full. You will be like Ramzi who did not deny that his family went through hard times, but who declared that it is worth it. He said," It is worth it because we lived in darkness and ignorance, but now we have joy! We are seeing new things every day."

Do You Want The Life (Zoe) Of God?

Are you willing to take up your cross (whatever comes your way for following Christ obediently)?

Are you willing to let go of your psyche (man produced life) to serve Him?

Are you willing to keep moving ahead doing His will in your life, even in difficulty, with His help?

If you are willing to do that, you are *starting out right*!

If you have never received Jesus as your lord and savior, pray this prayer.

Lord Jesus, I admit that I am a sinner. Thank you for dying to pay the penalty for my sins. Would you forgive me of my sins and come into my life in order to be my Savior? I now give my life completely to you. You are my Lord. Fill me with Your Holy Spirit. With Your help, I will now follow you.[xliii] *If you have done this, contact me at the email in the endnote.*

If you are a believer in the lord Jesus but have never turned your life over to Jesus pray the following:

Lord Jesus, thank you for forgiving my sins and saving me. I want the full life that You have for me. Therefore, I give my life to You. Be my Lord! Guide me and empower me. Fill me with the Holy Spirit and use me. (See endnote iii at the end of the chapter on ways to contact John Shuey and get materials to help you grow in your faith.)

This is the way to start your walk with the Lord. Making this decision to follow Christ is the only way to begin our quest to follow Him. If we have not settled ahead of time that we will follow Him no matter what, we may become disillusioned and quit when things are tough. I remember reserving a room at a university in Pennsylvania to meet some students who were interested in hearing about Christ or receive discipleship training. I was the only one who showed up. Not one other person. I sat outside the room after quite a bit of time had passed and felt like quitting. As I sat there, feeling sorry for myself, I thought, "If I quit here, I will want to do the same thing somewhere else." If you commit yourself fully to Him, you are more likely keep going when things become difficult.

The Remainder Of The Book

If you have been startled, as I was, by Paul's statement that we will access the inheritance of Jesus (being heirs together with Him) if we suffer, then you may wonder if Paul has given any instruction to assist us as we experience the difficulties that we face, either because of everyday life or because we suffer for following Christ. As I read that passage with new eyes that day, I made another amazing discovery. Immediately, after Paul informed them that they would need to suffer, he spent the next 22 verses giving them some mindsets and principles to assist believers not only to cope with the suffering they will experience, but also to keep help them keep plowing, so they will be able to say with him: *"I have fought the fight, I have finished the race..."* (2 Timothy 4:8). We will now spend time looking at five key passages in Romans 8:18-39 that will help us keep moving forward during difficult times.

CHAPTER SIX
Consider the Outcome

Ali was a jihadi whose brother had become a Christian. One day, Ali met a girl on the bus who told him not to talk with her because she was Christian, a very dangerous admission. Because Ali liked the girl, he told her that his brother was a Christian. As she became comfortable with Ali, she asked if his brother could get her a Bible. Ali got her a Bible but before he gave it to her, he became curious and began to read it. He had many questions as he compared the Bible with the Qur'an.

One night, Ali had a dream[xliv] where Jesus spoke to him and said, "Come to me all who are heavy burdened, and I will give you rest." When Ali woke up, he said, "Lord, forgive me. You are Christ. You are God and I believe." He eventually married the girl and they have become church planters. He is often interrogated by the police and shares his testimony when they ask him questions about how he could have been a jihadi and now a Christian. He says, "Honestly, the Christian life is a painful life," but he lives in undiminished joy, saying," When I die, I know where I am going."[xlv]

It seems that one of the ways that Ali handles the difficulties of his sufferings is to realize that they are temporary, because some day he will be with Jesus in heaven. Interestingly, the first thing Paul encourages us to do when we experience the difficulties, is to focus upon our eternal destiny. He says, *"I consider that our present sufferings are not worth comparing with the glory that will be revealed in us" (Romans 8:18).* As we have already noted, Paul experienced a great deal of suffering, ranging from personal physical difficulties and shipwrecks, to beatings and imprisonment for the faith. When he says, "I consider," he is evaluating his situation by making a comparison.[xlvi] As with Ali above, Paul concludes that "what I have experienced is hard. However, when things get tough, I think about my future." I think of the good God is going to do, and I especially think about what life will be like in eternity, and I conclude that I can endure this. I can endure this because I am headed toward an indescribable future. Suffering becomes easier when I *consider the outcome*. He asks us to do the same when we suffer.

The Earthly Outcome

Although I believe that Paul had his eternity in view when he talked about the glory to be revealed, he may have had his attention, in a small part, on the here and now. He says, *"And we, who with unveiled faces all reflect the Lord's glory, are being transformed into his likeness with ever-increasing glory, which comes from the Lord, who is the Spirit" (2 Corinthians 3:18).* As believers in the Lord Jesus Christ, we have access to His presence! We can get to know Him! The apostle John tells us that when we see him we will become more and more like Him (1 John 3:2). Before we knew Christ, we had no hope of overcoming sin and becoming more righteous. Now we know Christ, and as we seek to obey Him, we are becoming more like Him every day. We are moving from one degree of glory to another. Hallelujah!

Before we came into a relationship with Christ, we could not imagine assisting in God's plan to redeem the world. As we become more like Him, we will become more effective in fulfilling the plan that He designed for us before the creation of the world (Ephesians 2:10). Now, He uses us in the lives of others. This is glorious as well.

As we will see in Chapter Eight, God even leverages our suffering to produce good in and through our lives.

<u>The Eternal Outcome</u>

In addition to the present, Paul has the eternal in mind. He says, "When I consider all the difficulties that I have had in my life because 'life happens' in this decaying world and I am frequently opposed for ministering the Gospel, I conclude that these are nothing compared to what eternity holds for me." Let us explore what eternity will be like.

For someone to become a professional athlete, he or she must have a great deal of natural talent. They will have to go through a great deal of pain and intense workouts that include cardio and weight training. They work thousands of hours to develop the skills necessary for their sport. They will work through injuries and times of discouragement. They do this to get a paycheck, but more than anything they do it so they can win a gold medal or hoist a championship trophy. When they are going through difficulties, they ponder what it will be like to be a champion. They would tell you that all the workouts, body aches and sacrifices were not worth comparing the feeling of being champion. As we said in the last chapter, sporting achievements are temporary, but we are living for the Lord who gives us an eternal prize.

In the remainder of this chapter, we will look at some key passages that talk about what our eternity with God will be like. I will do my best to describe what the Scriptures say to us about eternity. There is no way to describe the eternal when we only have finite words and finite minds. It is inadequate at best. Eternity will be better than it is described here, but as you will see, what we do know is absolutely mind-blowing!

What Kind Of Environment Will We
Live In For Eternity?

In the remainder of the chapter, I will talk about three aspects of our life in eternity. I will save the best for last! Let's begin by talking about the environment of our eternal home. When I first became a Christian, it seemed that this was the area that most Christians discussed when they talked about going to be with Jesus. So, we will begin there. I will be using some larger portions of Scripture in this chapter, and will not include the entire passage, but would ask you to spend some time reading these passages prior to reading my material. I know that this seems like a lot, but we are talking about getting our sights set on eternity, so that we can victoriously endure life's struggles at us as we seek to follow the Lord. Remember the athlete who gets up early to work out and stays up late to look at videos of opponents, just to get a little edge. Should we not be willing to do the same so we can glorify our Lord? Our passage for this part of the chapter is Revelation 21:1-22:5.

Although we will go back to the beginning of Revelation 21, I want to begin with verse 7:

He who overcomes will inherit all this, and I will be his God and he will be my son (Revelation 21:7).

The Apostle John tells us that the one who inherits all that is being talked about is the one who overcomes (Greek *nikao*). *Nikao* means to "conquer, overcome, prevail, get the victory.[xlvii] So it seems that all the eternal blessings that we are going to discuss in this chapter are being reserved for the ones who fulfill the will of God, despite the hardships, afflictions, sufferings and persecutions that we have discussed in the first part of the book. This verifies what Paul told us in Romans 8:17. We will be joint heirs with Christ, if we suffer with Him. Let's begin to look at some of the wonderful benefits that will come to those who overcome.

There will be a new heaven and a new earth (Revelation 21:1-2).

The old order that was corrupted by the Fall will no

longer exist. Peter goes into more detail about the destruction of the old order when he tells us that the elements in both heaven and earth will be destroyed by fire (2 Peter 3:10). The old order will give way to a brand new heaven and earth, which will be a place of righteousness. We really cannot imagine what this will be like, however, John tells us that the New Heaven and New Earth will be like a bride prepared for her husband. The goal of every bride is to be more beautiful than she has ever been on her wedding day. Can we image that God would do any less?

Indeed, if it is possible for God to outdo Himself, which it is not, He did! Listen to the description of the city. It was in a cube, meaning that it is as wide as it is long and as it is high. It is about 1500 miles in each direction. It has twelve gates that are always open, each made of a single pearl and having the names of the twelve tribes on them. The foundation has the names of the twelve apostles and is covered with a variety of precious stones. The walls were made of jasper and the city is pure gold and the streets are made of translucent gold. It is an awesome place!

The dwelling of God will be with men (Revelation 21:3).

There is no temple in the city. It is not necessary, because God Himself is there. His glory provides the light for the city, so it is never dark. We will talk in more detail about being in the presence of God later in the chapter.

There will be no death or mourning or crying or pain.

"..._for the old order of things has passed away" (Revelation 21:4). We live in a place impacted by the Fall. We have emotional and physical pain caused by sickness, heartache, and rejection. Both can come from being unable to cope with the difficulties that life throws at us. In this life, we mourn the loss of loved ones, jobs, personal skills, abilities, and many other things, and ultimately we all experience death. In the new order of things, there will be no pain, no loss and no death. There will be no reason to cry or to mourn. What a truth to meditate upon when we are going through pain! Yes, pain exists now, but someday it will be no more. As I am writing, I have pain that is under the surface most of the time, but becomes more intense at times because of a broken relationship. It is great to look forward to a day when there will be no emotional or physical pain.

Sinners will not be there (Revelation 21:8, 27).

Later in this chapter, we will talk about what God does to transform us from sinner to a perfected person of God. In the New Heaven and New Earth, we will not have any people who are idolaters, immoral, or engaged in witchcraft. Those who choose this lifestyle will be in the lake of fire. This means that no one will be there who can convince us to sin or to reject God in any way. It means that we will not have a corrupt culture that can persuade large numbers to rebel against God and do wrong things. We will be in contact with other people who will walk in righteousness and have a heart to worship and serve the Lord.

There will be no curse.

We are told that there is a river going through the city with fruit bearing trees on either side. These will be for the healing of the nations. This will fulfill the command that God gave to Adam and Eve in the original Garden of Eden to be fruitful and multiply and fill the earth and subdue it. There will be no curses that arise because of disobedience. There will be no disobedience.

Inhabitants of the New Heaven and the New Earth will see God's face and His Name will be written on their foreheads.

We will talk more of seeing His face later in this chapter, but to have His Name on our foreheads means that we belong to Him and we are His servants. I believe that we will have responsibilities in eternity because we have been created to fulfill a purpose. That sounds exciting to me! We could not be complete without fulfilling the role that God has for us.

We truly cannot imagine what this will be like, but it is much better than anything we have on earth. Is this enough to motivate us to be conquerors, by finishing the work that God has given us to do even though we suffer? Amazingly, we are only getting started, as we get a glimpse of what eternity will be like.

What Will We Be Like In Eternity?

We have already gotten a hint of what we will be like from the Revelation passage. We certainly will not be engaging in sin or idolatry, and will probably have significant, fulfilling responsibilities. In this section, we will be looking at 1 Corinthians 15. Again, I encourage you to read the chapter before you proceed. It will help to imbed the truths in your mind for when you need the encouragement later.

Paul begins this passage by focusing upon the Gospel. It is simply that Christ died for our sins in order to purchase salvation for us, and He rose from the dead in order to provide a new life for us. He begins by spending time talking about those who had seen the resurrected Christ. He says that Jesus appeared to Peter, then the Twelve, to 500 at one time and eventually to James. Paul then reminds his readers that he met Christ on the Damascus road. He talked about those who had seen Christ after the resurrection because:

> *If there is no resurrection of the dead, then not even Christ has been raised. And if Christ has not been raised, our preaching is useless and so is your faith* (1 Corinthians 15:13-14).

If Jesus did not rise from the dead, then He did not enter the presence of His Father with His blood to purchase our salvation once for all (see Hebrews 9:11-12).

In addition, if Christ did not rise from dead then neither will anyone else. Paul concludes that if believers are not raised with Christ, then they are to be pitied more than anyone because we lived our whole life denying ourselves what this world has to offer, expecting to be with Christ in the New Heaven and New Earth, and we are going into the ground like everyone else. He says that it also means that all of our preaching is useless, and we are still in our sins. However, Paul says, "He did rise from the dead. Over 500 can attest to it! I can attest to it! I did meet Him on the road to Damascus." As a result, all who have received Christ in their lives as Lord and Savior will be resurrected some day. Now, let's take a look at what that will be like.

Before we get to what we will be like in eternity, we must look at two other important aspects of Christ's resurrection mentioned by Paul:

He will destroy all dominion, authority and power (1 Corinthians 15:24-25).

Jesus is going to reign until He has defeated all His enemies. When He does that, He will hand the entire Kingdom to His Father.

The last enemy to be defeated will be death (1 Corinthians 15:25).

We will be alive eternally. We will truly be alive with that "*zoe*" life!

Let's talk about what we as believers will be like for all eternity.

Although we are corruptible on earth, we will be raised incorruptible.

So will it be with the resurrection of the dead. The body that is sown is perishable, it is raised imperishable (1 Corinthians 15:42).

While we are in this life, we slip up. We are corruptible. We see that in our world and in our own culture. We can be lied to, deceived, and taken down a bad path. (Thankfully, as believers, we have the help of the Holy Spirit and we can walk in the victory He gives). In eternity, there will be no one there to negatively influence and corrupt us, and we will not be able to be corrupted. There will be no evil desires, no temptation, and no devil. What a place and what a transformation in our personal life!

Our body is sown in dishonor and raised in glory (1 Corinthians 15:43).

Our bodies are in dishonor because we can and have sinned. We have brought dishonor to God and we have brought dishonor to ourselves. We will be raised in glory. Dr. John Gill tells us that being raised in glory means that it is "in perfect beauty and comeliness, without the least blemish, defect, or imperfection; nor will there be any part of it that will occasion shame;"[xlviii] We are perfect, and we can't be corrupted.

Our body is sown in weakness and raised in power (1 Corinthians 15:43).

On earth we are diseased, or infirm, in our spirit, soul and body. Physically, death will come. We are raised in power. The word used for "power" means that we will have ability. We will not be sick or weak -- emotionally or spiritually.

Our body is sown a natural body and is raised a spiritual one (1 Corinthians 15:44).

Adam Clarke says that we are "no longer dependent on natural productions for its support."[xlix] There can be no decay and our spiritual being will control everything.

We live in a natural, corrupt body which is weak and can cause shame on this earth. However, if we know the Lord Jesus Christ, we no longer need to feel death's sting. Death is not the end. It is the beginning, a beginning where we will live in the amazing New Heaven and New Earth with a body that cannot be corrupted, is not weak, does not experience shame and is controlled by the Spirit. Death is not something that brings a sting to believers, because death ushers us into perfection. We merely leave earth to go into our eternal home where we will walk in perfection. However, there is one more aspect of our eternity which we have not talked about yet, and it is the best part!

We will be in his presence, beholding his glory for all eternity

Kerry and I have had the privilege of ministering in India seventeen times. Many times, when we traveled from the airport to our hotel, I sat there in silence observing the city of Mumbai. I was continually drawn to look at the sights that are so different than what I am used to in the U.S. However, no matter how interesting the sights, the best part was to see our friends. Usually, our friend Sanjay would pick us up at the airport. As we went from city to city, we would once again catch up with people who had become our friends. We have many wonderful and fun memories that I would love to share with you, but, alas, there is no space.

The New Heaven and New Earth will be amazing! I am sure that we could spend eternity exploring the intricacies of its beauty. However, I believe that the greatest blessing will be to observe God in all of His glory. We have already seen that we will see His face (Revelation 22:4). Albert Barnes tells us that seeing his face means, "They would be constantly in his presence, and be permitted continually to behold his glory."[1] During our time on earth, we have only been able to get veiled glimpses of Him as described inadequately in the Word.

We have been limited, as was Moses when he asked God to show him His glory (Exodus 33:18-23). God told Moses that

He would take him to a cleft in the rock and cover Moses' face, because no one (on earth) can see His face and live. God enabled Moses to see HIs goodness passing by. We have certainly seen His goodness. We have been forgiven of sin. We have been changed by the indwelling Holy Spirit. We have been given peace, joy, and purpose. We have been sustained in difficulty. He has been, and is, good! However, when we are changed, when we take on the incorruptible, powerful, spiritual body, we will be able to continually gaze into His face and observe His glory. Will we even notice the New Heaven and the New Earth, or will we be fully enraptured by His glory?

We can only meditate on what it will be like to observe His glory. Scripture, however, does give us some glimpses into His glory. These are incomplete, but should be enough to cause us to long to be with Him. These veiled glimpses of His glory will also serve to help us to hold on in difficulty, because we know that our time on earth, our time of suffering, is for a "short" time, but being with Him will be forever.

When we see God, in all of His glory, we will observe, Father, Son and Holy Spirit, the One God in three persons.[li] The knowledge that He is One, but yet three, is a beginning point of our wonder of the grandeur of God, even on earth. How can He be three, yet one? This is beyond our comprehension. Yet He would not be God if we could figure Him out. He is beyond us in character, power, wisdom, love, and everything else. Even on earth, we must conclude that He is awesome!

Our goal today is to attempt to grasp what God is like in His Glory, in order to motivate us to so look forward to seeing Him that way, that it enables us to endure suffering on earth. The Scriptures do give us some glimpses into God's heavenly glory.

The Scriptures only give us a small glimpse of God. He can't fully communicate His glory to us and we can't fully grasp what He does reveal, but let us take a look at a few of these

Scriptures.

> *At once I was in the Spirit, and there before me was a throne in heaven with someone sitting on it. And the one who sat there had the appearance of jasper and carnelian. A rainbow, resembling an emerald, encircled the throne* (Revelation 4:2-3).

> *From the throne came flashes of lightning, rumblings and peals of thunder...* (Revelation 4:5).

> *Also before the throne there was what looked like a sea of glass, clear as crystal...* (Revelation 4:6).

We are awestruck by the throne that God will sit upon, but we also marvel at the fact that John couldn't properly describe the One sitting on the throne. As he describes the scene God gave him, he is grasping for some way to describe the One sitting on the throne. He basically says, "I can't tell you what He looked like, but let me give you the closest earthly description." He says, His appearance is like that of precious stones. The rainbow and precious stones indicate His beauty, and the flashes of lighting, His power. This was the best John could do. We will only know how close he got when we get there.

His presence and His actions illicit praise from every kind of being. First, we see four living creatures: one like a lion, another like an ox, a third like a man, and the last like an eagle. These cry out, *"Holy, holy, holy is the Lord God Almighty, who was and is and is to come..."* (Revelation 4:8). This is reminiscent of the scene in Isaiah 6, where the creatures cry out, *"Holy, Holy, Holy!"* When we are told that God is holy, it means that He is "other than" the created universe. As they cry out to Him, they are awestruck that He is unique and different than creation in every wonderful and inconceivable way. Saying once that He is "other than" us, in ways too awesome to communicate, is not enough. Twice was not enough. In each case, they had to say it three times. We see that getting a glimpse of Him sends every living being into spontaneous, passionate worship!

We have seen that these unique four beings worshiped God, but they are not the only ones. Immediately after the four beings cry, *"Holy, holy, holy!"* We find twenty-four elders who sit around the throne throw their crowns before the Lord and exclaim that He is worthy of honor and glory (Revelation 4:11). Their crowns would represent the rewards they had gained in their service to the Lord. They throw them at His feet because no one deserves honor but God alone. He is awesome!

Up until now, we have seen the heavenly beings praise God for who He is. Next, we see the four creatures and the elders praising God for what He has done. He is the only One worthy to open the scrolls, talked about in Revelation 5. He is worthy because the great salvation that He purchased has won men and women from every tongue, tribe and nation, delivering them from their sin and making them into a Kingdom of priests that impact the world for God (Revelation 5:9-10).

As these twenty-eight finish praising God, the angels around the throne get involved. We see 10,000 times 10,000, which, if taken literally, would be billions. I believe John is describing an uncountable number of angels worshipping Him. They cry out that the Lamb who was slain is worthy of honor and praise! Immediately after that, we are told that every creature in heaven on the earth and under the earth and in the sea declared, *"Amen!"* (Revelation 5:13-14). He alone is worthy!

It does not stop there. We also find that the redeemed from every tongue, tribe and nation were in white robes, indicating that they have been made clean, shouting, *"Salvation belongs to our God, who sits on the throne, and to the Lamb"* (Revelation 7:10).

He is indescribably great! On earth, we can't comprehend even a little of His glory. However, the Scriptures indicate that glory, manifested in His holy character and incredible actions, cause all manner of heavenly beings to worship Him in passionate, unabated praise. It seems as they get newer and newer looks at Him, they can't help themselves. Worship is the "natural" response!

Heaven Is A Wonderful Place!

At the beginning of the chapter, Paul said that when I go through suffering, I consider my suffering in light of what the future will be like. As we will see in future chapters, this includes ways that God changes us or uses us in the midst of suffering or after it has passed. The biggest calculation that Paul makes, however, is what eternity will be like. In eternity, we will live in the New Heaven and New Earth. Its luxury cannot be described. Its light is the glory of God. There will be no sinners there and there will be no mourning, crying or pain.

In addition, we will be changed. We will be incorruptible, powerful, and possess honor. More awesome than any of this will be that we will have continual contact with the Godhead: Father, Son and Holy Spirit. We will be awestruck by His power, beauty, and holiness. We will be so enraptured by His glory that we will fall before Him in continual worship.

Can This Help Us Hold On?

Athletes train hard to win a trophy! Adults go on drastic diets before they go to their high school reunion to show they have kept in shape. Students study to learn a trade or qualify for a job. They believe the discipline and pain are worth the results.

If people put up with "suffering" for these perishable things, can we keep moving ahead in our quest to serve the Lord and advance His Kingdom when we experience a natural disaster, sickness, rejection, or some type of persecution, knowing that we will be changed? Someday, we will take off the corruptible to live in a place of indescribable beauty where we will continually see our Savior in His magnificent glory forever and ever. As we go through difficulty, with the help of God's Spirit, let's seek to focus upon the wonderful eternity God offers to

those who suffer for His sake. It will take the edge off and help us
to get through.

CHAPTER SEVEN
"Where's God?"

Most of us are aware of Job's story. He lost his wealth and all ten of his children in one day. He responded in a godly way. Then, he lost his health and bore excruciating pain. It was so bad that his wife told him to curse God and die. Job responded righteously, even though he didn't understand what was going on. He had always sought to live his life properly, praying for his children and caring for the needy. Now this. He finally confessed that he cried out to God, but God didn't answer him. He only looked at him (Job 30:20).

Have you ever wondered where God is? You may be sitting in the emergency room with a sick child, or standing at the bedside of a dying parent or spouse. Perhaps you gave up everything to serve the Lord in some capacity in the church or in some international ministry, and you only received criticism and rejection. You may have been fired from your job or even a ministry post.

In the middle of it, you may have had friends like Job's. His friends assumed that Job must have had sin in his life, and that God was punishing him for that sin. Your friends may not have come right out and said it, but you knew they suspected that your pain was your fault.

Your pain may be the internal pain caused by your failure to obey God the way you want to. You long to be more like Christ but seem to fall short, or you want to share the Gospel but never take advantage of opportunities to do so.

In each of these cases, you may feel alone and even say, "God, where are you?" The pain that you are experiencing may be so deep, and your anguish so strong, that you almost feel like groaning.

A Whole Lot Of Groaning Going On

In Romans 8:18 we learned that it helps to look at our suffering in light of the glorious future that God has for us, because seeing what awaits us can motivate us to hang on for just a little longer. As we move on from verse 18, we see the word "groan" three times in verses 19-26.

Creation groans (Romans 8:19-22).

We have already talked about the fact that something happened to creation when Adam and Eve sinned. At that time, creation itself was impacted, causing it to fall short of what God had originally intended. It is less than its created perfection, and it is getting worse because of the corruption that has occurred. We are told that creation groans. Even creation knows that something is not right. Creation groans for the freedom of the children of God, because when God completely frees His children, there will be a New Heaven and a New Earth. Creation will be made perfect, as we already described in Chapter Six.

Humans groan (Romans 8:23-25).

We, as humans, groan as well. In some ways, all people groan because they know something is wrong. Something is wrong with a world that continually goes to war or participates in skirmishes. We know something is wrong when people are not valued because of the color of their skin, their gender, or religion. Yes, humans know something is wrong because of these, and many other things that they observe. This is especially true for those who know the Lord. In another letter Paul says:

However, as it is written: "No eye has seen, no ear has heard, no mind has conceived what God has prepared for those who love him"-- but God has revealed it to us by his Spirit. The Spirit searches all things, even the deep things of God (1Corinthians 2:9-10).

When we received Christ into our lives, we were born again because the Spirit of God came to live in us (Romans 8:9). When this happened, He began to point out to us the things that God prepared for us. As we began to recognize that we have fallen short of God's best, we also groan, desiring to be all that God is showing us that we can be, yet recognizing that we have some distance to go.

Paul openly groans at the end of Romans 7. He tells his readers that he does the things that he does not want to, and he does not do the things that he ought. He is groaning because he knows what God wants him to be, and longs for the day when his life begins to look more like the one God desires. He finally exclaims, "Who will deliver me from this body of death?" (Fortunately for Paul, he did not stay there. Romans 8 gives this answer.)

In addition, believers groan because they begin to understand how society and our world could be if the whole world would embrace Christ and allow Him to change individuals' lives and entire cultures.

The Spirit groans (Romans 8:26-27).

In the same way, the Spirit helps us in our weakness. We do not know what we ought to pray for, but the Spirit himself intercedes for us with groans that words cannot express. And he who searches our hearts knows the mind of the Spirit, because the Spirit intercedes for the saints in accordance with God's will (Romans 8:26-27).

The Holy Spirit, because He is God, knows all about us. He knows that God wants us to walk in holiness. He knows the plan that God ordained for us prior to the beginning of the world (Ephesians 2:10). He knows where we fall short. He knows what needs to happen in our lives to get us to where God wants us to be. He intercedes for us so that we overcome the past, and become what God wants us to become.

He also groans because He wants the entire world to know what God has prepared for it. He wants people from every tongue, tribe and nation to know Him and He wants them to allow Him to change their cultures into all that God wants.

Romans 8 also tells us that Jesus prays for us (see Romans 8:34; see also Hebrews 7:25, where we are told that Jesus lives forever to pray for us.)

So, where is God when we are going through suffering and when the heavens are like brass? He is praying for us! He is not just looking, as Job suspected. He is praying for us, even during those times that we are groaning in pain or groaning because we long to be more. In Psalm 10:1, David also wondered where God was, but he gives us great encouragement in the very next Psalm when he says:

> *"When the foundations are being destroyed, what can the righteous do?" The LORD is in his holy temple; the LORD is on his heavenly throne. He observes the sons of men; his eyes examine them.* (Psalms 11:3-4).

God is still in His holy temple! He is still on the throne! When you are tempted to wonder where He is, remember this; He is praying for us!

What Are Jesus And The Holy Spirit Praying For Us?

We are unable to tell exactly what Jesus and the Holy Spirit are praying for us, unless He specifically tells us.[lii] At times, the Holy Spirit will place a thought in our mind that we know is from Him. This may communicate how He is praying, since He is praying that we will comply with His leading. In addition, He may highlight a Scripture to us that convicts us of some sin that must be repented of or give us some insight into the direction He wants us to go. We can assume that if He is speaking to us about something, He is also praying for us in these areas.

There are some general areas where the Holy Spirit prays for each of us. I have not placed them in any particular order.

He prays that we will become all that God intends for us.

The Holy Spirit, who is God, knows and understands God's will and purpose for our life. He counseled with the Father and Son before time began, as they contemplated the time in which we would live, and the purpose that He would have for us. This fact alone should motivate us to worship God. We are not an accident in the timeline of history. God has been working His plan to bring everything under Jesus Christ (Ephesians 1:9-10). He knew exactly who He would need as His ministers during this time. He brought us into the world and gave us a specific role to play as He advances His Kingdom! Imagine that!

However, as we said earlier, God created us with free will. This means that we can resist God's call for us. We might be particularly inclined to resist God during times of suffering. We may feel forsaken or rejected by the Lord, and question whether we can trust Him. Frankly, we may be angry at the Lord when we are going through particularly difficult times. We may lack the physical and emotional energy to fight negative thoughts.

The Holy Spirit is praying for us all the time. I believe He is particularly praying for us during times when we are suffering, since we might be disillusioned or just focused upon solving our problems. His prayer is especially important because Satan or one of his emissaries will seek to use the sickness or rejection to get us to walk away from the Lord. In the next chapter, we will see that God often leverages our suffering to accomplish good in or through us. Satan, however, seeks to use our suffering to get us to distrust the Lord and walk away from God's plan.

I mentioned earlier that Kerry went through a very painful situation in a close personal relationship which hindered her from focusing upon preparation for a trip to Africa for quite some time. Satan wanted her to become so distraught that she would be unable to continue to minister as she had previously done. God, however, used it to take her deeper with Him, to show her how to have peace in the middle of pain and to give her a ministry in the lives of many others who are experiencing the same pain in their life.

Joseph Tson was a well-known preacher in Romania. When he was told not to preach, he did. He was brought before authorities and interrogated, sometimes ten hours per day. He said that when you are suffering, your question should not be "Why?" but rather, "God, what do you want to do in the world through my suffering?"[liii] God does have a purpose. The Holy Spirit is praying that we will walk with God in our suffering so God can fulfill His will in the situation.

The Holy Spirit is praying, first all of all, that we come to know Jesus Christ as our Lord and Savior. He not only prays for us to come into a relationship with Jesus, but He is intimately involved in the process of drawing us to Him. On Jesus' last night, prior to His crucifixion, He told the disciples that when He went back to be with the Father, He would send the Holy Spirit, who would convince the world (those who do not know Jesus) of sin, righteousness and judgment. In other words, He would be showing people that they are sinners that fall short of the righteous requirement of God and, as a result, are facing judgment. The Holy Spirit does this to show unbelievers they have a need for Christ so they will seek Him in much the same way that an oncologist tells a patient they have cancer so they will seek treatment. If we do not receive Christ and follow Him, we will never reach our full potential.

I remember the night that I was sitting in church, and an evangelist shared how we needed to receive Christ in our life in order to live the right life and avoid eternal judgment. At the time, I was not one who would respond publicly, but I went to the front of the church to demonstrate my need for Christ, and to receive Him into my life. Looking back, I believe that the Holy Spirit was praying that I would give up my pride and respond to Him.

Once we come into a relationship with Jesus, the Holy Spirit is praying that we will develop the character of Jesus. As He prays this, He is really praying that we will walk in step with His leading, demonstrating the results (fruit) of living in Him:

> *But the fruit of the Spirit is love, joy, peace, patience, kindness, goodness, faithfulness, gentleness, and self-control. Against such things there is no law"* (Galatians 5:22-23).

He is praying that we will allow Him to control our lives, because if we do not, we will not act differently than we did before we asked Christ to come into our life. The Holy Spirit wants us to live the life God created us to live, so He prays that we walk with Him.

He not only prays that we will develop the character of Jesus, but He prays that we will discover and fulfill the ministry plan He has for us. Again, He not only prays for us to discover and fulfill the role He has for us, but He comes alongside us to help us, if we allow Him to. Jesus told His disciples to wait until they received power from the Holy Spirit before they began their ministry. As we allow the Holy Spirit to help us in ministry, He empowers the words that we speak for Him, and uses our actions for Him to impact people's lives in a way that advances Christ's Kingdom. (See Acts 1:8 and Acts 2:1 ff.).

As we have said repeatedly, God has a specific plan for each of our lives. (Remember Ephesians 2:10). It is our calling. Some are called to vocational ministry. Others have been called to work a "secular"[liv] job and minister at their workplace. Still others are called to work in their local church. Many will work in their job and serve in the church. Some are called to teach and lead, and others are called upon to serve. The Holy Spirit is guiding us so that we find and pursue our God-ordained calling. He is also praying that we will discover our place of ministry and the spiritual gifts that enable us to minister effectively. The Holy Spirit is involved with us and prays for us during every step of our life.

He prays that we will make it through our suffering.

You may wonder why I did not begin here since the book is about walking with God through suffering. I did this because we must get a glimpse of where we are going before we can stay on course during difficulty. The ancient plowman focused upon a tree or some landmark on the other side of the field so he would plow a straight line. We must understand that the Holy Spirit has a plan for us. That plan is the landmark we focus upon as we suffer. We keep this in mind as we seek to make sense of, and get through, our hardship. The overall goal is that He wants us to know Jesus, be like Jesus, and advance the Kingdom of Jesus. As we consider *finishing strong*, we must understand that we are seeking to finish the plan God has for us. Someone said, "If you do not have a goal, you will hit it every time!" God has a destination for us. When the Holy Spirit prays for us to make it through difficulty, He is praying that we walk through the suffering and get to the other side in a way that keeps us moving toward God's goal for us. He wants us to keep plowing.

We see this in the case of Peter. Peter had denied that he knew Jesus three times, as Jesus was going through His trial. Satan planned to take Peter out that night. Jesus told Peter that Satan was going to go after him, but He said, "I have prayed for you." (Luke 22:31-32) I hate to think of what might have happened, had Jesus not prayed for Peter. Jesus and the Holy Spirit are also praying for us as we go through hardship and pain. They are praying that we will learn any lessons we are to learn (we will discuss this in the next chapter), keep moving ahead as much as we can during the trial and finish the race that He has for us.

He prays that we will make right decisions.

We make decisions each day which determine whether we will fulfill God's plan for our life, or not. As we make those decisions, the Holy Spirit is praying for us because they have an impact upon us *finishing strong*.

...as we experience temptation.

Each of us experiences temptation. The good news is that with temptation, God provides a way of escape: "

> No temptation has seized you except what is common to man. And God is faithful; he will not let you be tempted beyond what you can bear. But when you are tempted, he will also provide a way out so that you can stand up under it. (1 Corinthians 10:13)

When we are tempted, there is a way of escape. Maybe it's because I don't look for it, but I sometimes don't see the way of escape. I believe that the Holy Spirit sees us when we are tempted, and is praying for us. This ought to encourage us. He is praying that we will see the way of escape and take it. His prayers for us to avoid temptation in times of suffering are crucial. It is during these times that we can be prone to become bitter, or be more susceptible to engaging in activities that we might not generally be tempted to engage in, because they may provide a distraction or make us feel better for a period of time.

...as we make every decision.

We make decisions all the time. Some are smaller, like "Where do I buy groceries? or "What cloths should I wear?" Unless God has some divine appointment that day, these decisions may not have much impact, but we make far more consequential decisions on a regular basis: "Where should I live or work or attend church?" "Who should I marry?"... Many of these decisions will have a great impact upon my life. I can think of many decisions that I made that changed my life in ways that I would never have imagined. I choose my college. It was there that I met the man who provided discipleship training for me that lead me into future full-time ministry.

Let me tell you about a decision that set in motion a series of events leading to our ministry today. I served as pastor in a church that was a very difficult place for us. My wife felt we should move on much earlier than we did, but I dug in, not thinking it was the right time. One afternoon, we received a piece of mail that caused both of us to recognize that we were being released from that ministry, so we tendered our resignation, not knowing what we would do. We were both interested in prayer and missions ministries. At the same time that we resigned from the church, the Director of Prayer and Missions resigned from a large church in our area that was led by a friend of mine. After attending the church for awhile, not looking to be hired for the position, the elders asked us to come on staff to head up their missions and prayer departments.

While at that church, we went to a conference that gave a workshop outlining how to help believers get past bondage in their lives. This led to the development of our *Breaking Free to Your Destiny* course.[lv] After teaching our *Breaking Free* course at a module for the College of Prayer International, we were invited to serve on the Leadership Committee for College of Prayer International for a time, which opened the door for us to travel to India, Pakistan, Norway and Burkina Faso.[lvi]

While serving at the same church, we met others who opened doors of ministry in Romania, Liberia, W. Africa, Belgium, Austria, Slovakia, Slovenia, and Czech Republic. In addition, we traveled to Indonesia and Nicaragua with that church.

Because of our involvement with this church, we were asked to oversee a prayer ministry in the state of Pennsylvania. The one decision to transition from one church and go to another changed the trajectory of our lives. I believe that the Holy Spirit prayed for us and orchestrated the timing of our decision to line up future ministries.

My wife and I both believe that God used her desire to leave earlier than me and my desire to stay a bit longer to release us from that church at the right time. Paul told the Galatians, "*...But when the time had fully come, God sent his Son, born of a woman, born under law*" (Galatians 4:4). God chose the perfect time for Christ to come. He does the same thing in our lives.

You may wonder what this has to do with suffering. Because the situation in the church that we left was so painful, and it had been difficult for almost the entire eight years we served there, we could have decided to look for another position at an earlier time. I have to believe that the Holy Spirit prayed for us that we would hang in there until it was the right time. The timing was not only best for us, but for the entire congregation. When we are in a difficult situation, all of us might be tempted to make quick or ill-advised decisions. We need to follow His guidance. He knows what is best and when it is best. We must especially trust Him when we are experiencing difficulty, but be assured, He is praying for us that we will make the right decisions!

He prays that we will get revelation.

When Paul wrote to the church at Ephesus, he prayed that they would get a revelation:

> *"I keep asking that the God of our Lord Jesus Christ, the glorious Father, may give you the Spirit of wisdom and revelation, so that you may know him better"* (Ephesians 1:17).

He goes on to name three specific areas where he wants them

to gain revelation. We need to make very clear that when we speak of revelation here, we are not talking about new truths revealed in our day that are equal to Scripture, but rather that some truth of Scripture becomes so clear and real that it becomes truth the I live by.

As we hear sermons, attend Bible Studies and read the Scriptures, we gain an intellectual understanding of God's Word, but do we believe these truths enough to obey them when our reputations, finances or lives are on the line? After my junior year of college, I was given the opportunity to move to Madison, Wisconsin to participate in a Christian discipleship program. Participants in the program would get jobs during the daytime in order to pay room, board and other expenses. The bottom line is that if I did this, I would save very little money for my college expenses that summer. I went, knowing that I would be on my own for college expenses the next year, because I chose not to stay home and work that summer. One day, as I was pondering this decision, I had a picture in my mind. I saw myself sitting on the branch of a tree. All of a sudden, I began to saw off the branch that I was sitting on. The Lord said to me (not audibly)," I am asking you go to the training program. If you can't trust me to catch you after you have cut through the branch, you will really be wasting the rest of your life." I went to the training program and God met my needs. Truth is only revelation when we believe it so strongly that we obey.

Each of us needs to have Scripture etched into our minds and spirits. It needs to be so real to us that we live as though it is true, which it is. The Holy Spirit is praying that we will continually get Scriptures into our life that will energize faith and change our life.

We may gain a great deal of revelation while suffering, because we are open to whatever the Lord may say to us. Josef Tson said, "During the time I was expecting to be crushed by the Romanian secret police interrogator, God became more real to me than ever before or after in my life. It is difficult to put into words the experience I had with God at that time. It was like rapture into a sweet and total communion with the Beloved. God's test for me then became a pathway to special knowledge of the reality of God."[lvii]

It is possible when we suffer to begin to doubt God. The devil would like that to happen. As the Holy Spirit sees that we are struggling, He prays for us. He knows what we are going through, and He prays that we will get a revelation of truth from God so that we overcome and keep moving forward.

Where Is God?

Where is God when we cry out to Him and He does not seem to answer? He is not just looking. Jesus and the Holy Spirit see us clearly. They understand our situation and they know where they are leading us, and they continually pray for us. They pray that we will get through the sickness, persecution, affliction or hardship in a way that will enable us to know God better, grow in our personal life and become more effective in serving Him.

In the last two chapters, we have already seen that if we focus upon eternity and recognize that He is praying for us as we go through difficulty, we will be helped to keep plowing, even in our present undesirable circumstances. In the next chapter, we will discuss how God brings good out of our difficult circumstances.

CHAPTER EIGHT
Our Suffering Cooperates With God

Soro and Ali[lviii] had been out of Iran and had returned. They began to share Christ with their family and a number of them came to know Jesus. It was safe to reach family, but they began to reach others. When authorities began to notice, they were both imprisoned. Soro was eventually released after interrogation. When considering her imprisonment, she said, "He was allowing us, His children, to suffer because He wanted us to carry His presence into their presence. He loves them so much - the judge, the interrogators, the guards - that He allowed us to go through a really, really hard time so they could come in touch with Him." Before going home to await trial, she had the opportunity to pray with one of the prison officials. When she returned for her trial, she spent forty-five minutes telling her story: really, Christ's story.

Soro understood the third truth that Paul reveals, designed to assist us to navigate our way through suffering in a way that enables us to continue to fulfill His will for our life. The principle is this: God works good in bad situations. Paul has already told us that looking at the length and wonders of eternity helps us to hang on to God's purposes in our life. Life here is for a short time in comparison, and what I am looking forward to is infinitely greater than my suffering here. Secondly, he told us that when we are suffering, even though we do not see Him, the Holy Spirit prays for us with great passion that we will become all that God wants us to become, and that we will accomplish all that He has called us to fulfill.

Paul now reminds us of another important truth that will assist us to keep plowing in our walk with God during times of hardship. *"And we know that in all things God works for the good of those who love him, who have been called according to his purpose"* (Romans 8:28). The verb *"know"* is in the perfect tense.[lix] The perfect tense describes something that happened in the past and continues to have an impact on us today. For example, in 1989, I graduated from seminary. Those three and a half years (yes, I managed to squeeze a three-year program into three and one-half years) have continued to have an impact on my life and my ministry. The skills I developed there help me to this day (such as having an understanding of what the Greek perfect tense means). Basically, Paul is telling his readers, "I am sharing a truth with you that you already knew. Because you know this truth, it is helping you even today." We might say, "How does it help me to know that God produces good out of even bad situations?" It is because we know God. He is love! He is good! He is working in our life! Therefore, we know that He is working positive things in our lives, even when we can't see them.

The principle that they know is *"in all things God works for good."* The KJV tells us that *"all things work together for good."* The KJV captures the meaning of the original here. The word "works" (NIV) and "work together" (KJV) comes from a root word that means to be a "fellow-worker " or " to co-operate".[lx] This means that "all things" cooperate with God in order to accomplish good things.

This promise, says Paul, is for those who love God and are called according to His purpose. If we take a look at the next two verses, we find that these promises are for those who are justified. They have come into a relationship with Him and are called to His purposes. When we come into a relationship with Jesus, God calls us to fulfill the purpose which we have been created to complete. So, if we have come to know Him, then God works in every situation to bring us to the point where He fulfills His plan through us.

God performs these good things for those who love Him. We may cry, "foul." Why does God only bring good to those who love Him? The reason is that God accomplishes good in our life when we trust Him in our difficulty. As we trust Him in difficulty, we will obey Him and do what He wants of us to do, going where He wants us to be, (the place where the good takes place). If we trust Him, we will be less prone to bitterness, which, we will see in a later chapter, destroys the good things that God has for us. Solomon tells us:

> *Trust in the LORD with all your heart and lean not on your own understanding; in all your ways acknowledge him, and he will make your paths straight"* (Proverbs 3:5-6).

A child will be much more willing to jump into deep water if daddy is standing in the water to catch her, because she loves him and trusts him.

Paul asks, "Are you going through suffering? I've got news for you. God has a pleasant surprise waiting for you! He is going to bring something good out of your situation." You may look at a current situation and wonder how good can come out of it. You may be suffering from a severe illness or be without a job. One or more of your children might have rejected the Lord and live in rebellion to Him. You may have recently lost a loved one and don't know what you are going to do without them. You may have given your life to ministering for the Lord and have received push back and rejection. We could give many more scenarios. As we ponder each one, we may wonder how something good could come from it.

In the remainder of the chapter and the next, we will discuss some general ways that God uses difficulty to bring good in our lives, but before we experience the good that God brings from suffering, we must commit ourselves fully to God. As we said in Chapter Five, Jesus died to take us out of the old life and bring us into the fullness of the life He has purchased for us when He died on the cross, rose from the grave, and went back to be with the Father. When we commit ourselves to Him, we tell Him, "I believe that you know best! You know what I need at this time in my life and I trust you." Therefore, I *will* trust you." When we go through difficulty, we may ask Him as our loving Father, "what are you doing?" He will tell us whenever it will help us to walk through it, but sometimes He can't because we would not understand. When we get no answer, we need to follow Him, believing He will work his perfect will. We may eventually see at least some of the good that God has done, and, in some cases, we may not know until we go to be with Him.

God May Allow Suffering To Get Our Attention

King Saul wanted to kill David because David had become very popular, and he knew David (who was not his son) would someday be king. David decided to escape to Philistine territory so Saul would give up his pursuit. Saul did give up temporarily.

Later, the Philistines were lining up to fight against Saul, King of Israel. David and his men, who had been faithful to the Philistine King, Achish, came to the battle lines prepared to fight with him. However, Achish's commanders did not trust David because they believed he would turn against them to gain favor with Saul. David and his men were sent home to Ziklag. This was very painful for David and his men. David felt rejected because he had done much for Achish.

Imagine for a moment if David had fought with the Philistines. He would have been fighting on the wrong side. He would have been fighting against the armies of God. I believe that God caused David to be rejected to get his attention, to keep him from fighting on the wrong side. [lxi]

As a loving Father, God will seek, at times, to get our attention. Sometimes, He must use drastic and painful means to get it. I dated a young woman during my college years. We talked about marriage. She knew that I was interested in Christian ministry and was willing to be a pastor's wife, but when I shared with her that I was open to traveling overseas to serve as a missionary, she decided that she could not go that far from her family. I knew that I had to end the relationship, because I had to be open to God's will for my life, whatever that might be. It was extremely painful. It took a long time for me to get past this pain. God got my attention, for sure. She was not the person for me. When I met Kerry eight years later, I know why God had me break up with the young woman from college. He has a plan for us and wants us to fulfill that plan. Sometimes, He must put a roadblock in front of us in order to get our attention and keep us on course.

We talked earlier about the prophet Balaam. God tried to get his attention in a hilarious way. God had initially told Balaam not to go, when asked to prophesy against Israel. Balaam kept asking if he could, I believe, hoping to get the big payout. On one of his attempts to go, God had Balaam's donkey try to stop him. When Balaam got angry, the donkey talked to him. This is a bit freaky and would seem to have really gotten Balaam's attention. Unfortunately, Balaam was not deterred. Although he never did prophesy a negative word against Israel, he did tell Balak (the king who wanted him to curse Israel) how to get Israel to sin, thus causing God to have to curse Israel. Therefore, he got his big payday.[lxii] We must pay attention so God can get our attention!

The above stories tell us about God's efforts to get the attention of His people to keep them from getting off track.

God will also use events to call unbelievers to repentance, to bring them into a relationship with God. Perhaps the most famous of these incidents happened in the life of Saul of Tarsus, who became Paul, the Apostle to the Gentiles. Before he came to know Christ, he was hell-bent on stopping the fledgling church which he called the Way. He was on his way to Damascus to arrest believers and take them into custody. While he was on his way, a bright light surrounded him and the Lord Jesus, Himself, spoke to him. During the exchange, Paul was rendered blind for three days. Later, a Christian in Damascus, Ananias, led him to the Lord and prayed that he would be healed. He became the most prolific missionary, church planter of his day and perhaps of all time.[lxiii]

We find a number of instances in Revelation where God exclaims that the residents of earth did not repent after terrible pain (Revelations 9:20 and 16:9-11). This indicates that God loved the people of earth so desperately that He was willing to take drastic measures in order to wake up the people who have rejected Him in order to bring them to Himself.

Randy Alcorn tells the story of a woman who had a Christian upbringing but had rebelled against God. She realized she had made a mistake in rebelling against God when she was standing at her daughter's gravesite. She said:

On January 5, 2009, there by my daughter's gravesite, I asked Jesus into my heart. I prayed with a pastor of a local church we had never been a part of. I had thought about God a lot since that day. Taylor left this earth. The moment came at the burial, where I thought, this is it! I needed God right now! At that moment it all came to me, Taylor was sent here from God, to change my life, my husband's life and my entire family's life.[lxiv]

(These are her words, not mine or Randy Alcorn's).

We see the great love of God who is willing to allow events in our lives that we would never choose, to accomplish good in our lives. It is akin to an oncologist telling a patient the horrific news that he has cancer. He then tells him about a treatment plan that will cause his hair to fall out, sap his energy and cause him to be sick but, at the end, will give the patient many years of productive living. God is willing to do that for us in order to deal with the cancer of sin in our lives, so that we may get on track or stay on track. He has a purpose for our lives, and He will do what He needs to, so as to get us to fulfill it.

God Will Allow Suffering To Assist Us To Get To Know Him

My eye doctor had been encouraging me to have cataract surgery for a long time, but the idea of a sharp object going into my eye did not thrill me. Finally, when I couldn't properly decipher all the letters on my computer screen, I thought, "I need to have the surgery." After one eye was completed, I could not believe how bright and distinct the colors on my computer were. When I went outside, after the second eye was done, I said, "Wow! Why did I wait?" I now realize that when I looked into the sky, I saw everything in gray and two dimensional. I was amazed at the blue sky and the three-dimensional clouds. It still amazes me a number of years later. Previously, I had talked about the blue sky, but now I know it really is blue!

Sometimes, we must go through some suffering to truly get to know God. As we meet God in the middle of suffering, we get to see Him in action and get to know Him in reality, and not just intellectually.

Abraham is considered to be the father of the Jewish people. As such, he is the father of Christianity. Abraham's wife, Sarah, was unable to conceive children. God had promised Abraham that he would have an heir, but year after year went by with no child. Finally, Sarah had the idea that she would give her maiden, Hagar, to Abraham as a wife so that Hagar could have a child for him. Hagar did have a son, Ishmael, but God told Abraham that his heir would be Sarah's son. Finally, when Abraham was 99 and Sarah was 89, God said, "Next year, you will have your son." Lo and behold, the 90-year-old barren Sarah bore a son, Isaac, to Abraham. [lxv]

All God's promises to Abraham to impact the nations were tied up in Isaac. As Isaac moved toward adulthood, God told Abraham to take Isaac onto Mount Moriah and sacrifice Him on an altar. Now this seems like an unreasonable request, but Abraham set out to do it. As they got ready to go up the mountain, Abraham said that he and the boy would return, so he knew God was going to do something, but what?

Can you imagine the pain Abraham must have experienced as they moved up the mountain? He had prayed for this son all his life and now God is asking him to literally sacrifice him. The two of them got the whole way up the mountain, Abraham tied Isaac down, and raised his knife to kill him. Then God said, "Okay Abraham, you can stop." God had placed a ram in some bushes, which Abraham then sacrificed. We are told,

> *So Abraham called that place 'The LORD Will Provide.' And to this day it is said, 'On the mountain of the LORD it will be provided* (Genesis 22:14).

Before this event, Abraham believed in God as his provider, but now he knew God as provider in ways that he could not have imagined. Before this event, Abraham knew God, but after this event, it is as though he had spiritual cataract surgery. Once he saw a little, now he had a clearer revelation of God.

Randy Alcorn tells about a difficult year in the life of his wife, Nanci. He says that she spent the year in anxiety and fear even though no outside trauma sparked it. He says that all she could do during that time was to tell God how much she loved Him, morning, noon and night. She not only describes the year as one of fear and anxiety, but a year, "that made me fall in love with God."[lxvi] Alcorn says that the year of anxiety is over, but her sense of intimacy with God is not.

In the midst of his tremendous sufferings, Job developed a longing to see the Lord. I am sure that part of it had to do with the pain he was going through, but listen to him:

> *I know that my Redeemer lives, and that in the end he will stand upon the earth. And after my skin has been destroyed, yet*

> *in my flesh I will see God; I myself will see him with my own eyes-- I, and not another. How my heart yearns within me!* (Job 19:25-27)

As you look at the last phrase, we see that Job is not just looking for a way to be separated from his pain. He is longing to see Someone whom he loves. This longing occurred when He was in the middle of excruciating pain and unspeakable loss.

Believers down through the ages have experienced the power of God. In some cases, He has delivered them from a sin or a habit that had negatively impacted their life or the life of someone else. They experienced a healing touch from the Lord, like a missionary friend of mine. He had a debilitating case of diabetes that threatened to keep him from going to India. The Lord healed him and he spent thirty seven years ministering there. Out of his sickness, he saw God in a new way as the One who removes whatever obstacle is in the way of fulfilling the will of God.

Others have been sustained as they have watched a loved one go through sickness or death. They may not have seen the miracle they had hoped for, but God undergirded them in the most difficult time in their lives. The apostle Paul had some type of sickness or physical problem. He tells us that he prayed three times for God to take it away. After those three times, he concluded that it was not God's will to heal this particular situation. Paul tells us that the Lord told him,

> *My grace is sufficient for you, for my power is made perfect in weakness. Therefore I will boast all the more gladly about my weaknesses, so that Christ's power may rest on me"* (2 Corinthians 12:9).

Paul was not healed in this case. It isn't that Paul had not seen God work in miraculous ways. On one occasion, a very poisonous snake bit and latched onto Paul. Those present expected him to die almost immediately. He lived and had a great opportunity for ministry, including opportunities to see others healed (Acts 28:1-9). In the case of 2 Corinthians 12, Paul saw God's power through His sustaining grace. He saw the grace of God enable him to continue his rigorous ministry in spite of whatever the situation was. He saw the power of God manifested in His life, even when it was not through a healing miracle.

We too can get to know God better as we go through suffering, whether it be a sickness, trauma or rejection. We may see God perform a miracle which will enable us to see Him in amazing light, but we may also get to know Him when He takes us through a situation. We will see His compassion and love for us as He tenderly walks us through the difficulty. We see His strength as He helps us to endure difficulty. God takes the very thing that we do not want to experience and uses it to draw us closer to Him. He will use suffering to give us a revelation of Himself that will increase our love and worship of Him, and will energize our faith which will empower us to trust Him to fulfill His will in our life even when we are afflicted.

The truth is that there are aspects of God's character that we may never come to know apart from suffering. Martha and Mary suffered pain when their brother Lazarus died. They saw the compassion of Jesus as He wept over their brother. We may never see His ability to provide finances, or the companionship or skills of others, if we do not have a need. We may never see His power to change us if we do not experience anguish in an area where we need victory. When we go through difficulty (and no one wants to) let's get to know Him as best we can!

God Uses Suffering To Display His Works

God is glorified in everything that we will talk about in these two chapters. He is glorified when we come into a relationship with Him, even through suffering. He is glorified if He gets our attention and we are spared from walking in the wrong direction. He is glorified when we get to know Him better in the midst of suffering or through a miracle. As we will see in our next chapter, God is glorified when our character is changed through suffering, or when someone receives ministry from someone who knows their pain because they have felt similar pain. We will talk about these in detail in Chapter Nine.

In our last section, we talked about some ways that God has revealed Himself to individuals in such a way that it changed their lives. Some of these events, like God providing a sacrifice for Abraham, have been recorded in Scripture so this revelation of God has had an impact upon many others as well. The same could be said for others' stories that I have included. However, there are some events that are so amazing that they have been designed to demonstrate the glory of God in a way that catches the attention of many.

Jesus and His disciples came across and man who had been born blind. (John 9) The disciples (demonstrating some of the logic of Job's friends) asked Jesus who had sinned -- his parents, or the man himself. They assumed that no one would be born blind if it were not God's punishment. Jesus said, "neither of them sinned. He was born like this to display the works of God." Up until that point, no one who had been born without sight had ever had their sight restored, but Jesus healed Him! No one could deny that this was the hand of God. Many people took note. As a result, the religious leaders got involved in the situation. This was a miracle that was seen by many.

In the Old Testament, Elijah called for a contest with the priests of two false religions that had captured the hearts of many living in the northern tribes of Israel. (1 Kings 18). Elijah said, "Let's have a little contest and we will see who the true God is." He told the priest of the false gods to build an altar for a sacrifice and put a bull on it. Elijah said, "Do not light it." He wanted them to pray and ask their god, Baal, to light the fire, himself. After many hours, nothing happened. Elijah then took a bull and had them douse the bull and the place of sacrifice he had built with water, until the water flowed. He cried out to God and God lit the sacrifice. All who were there saw it and cried, *"The LORD--he is God! The LORD--he is God!"* (1 Kings 18:39). Again, the works of God had been displayed to a large number of people and had wide impact. Only God could do this. False gods, who are not really God, showed that they cannot do such a thing. God was therefore glorified!

At the same time as Elijah's challenge, Israel had been suffering terribly. They had been experiencing a drought, designed by God to get the attention of wicked King Ahab, King of the people of the northern tribes. There was no rain for years. They could not get feed for their animals. Elijah's contest happened in the middle of the drought. After the contest, he went out and prayed for rain and it rained. Both of these events had an impact on many.

God continues to do such a work in our day. Nick Vujicic was born with no arms or legs. His parents were devastated, having a crisis of faith, but they decided to trust God. Nick was bullied and rejected in school and could not quite understand that if God loved him, how could He make him like this. He considered suicide. Then he read the story of the man born blind and surrendered his life to Christ, desiring God to use his life for His glory. Nick says:

> Due to the emotional struggles I had experienced with bullying, self-esteem and loneliness, God began to instill a passion of sharing my story and experience to help others cope with whatever challenge they might have in their lives. Turning my struggles into something that would glorify God and bless others, I realized my purpose![lxvii]

I personally have a friend who pastors in a former Eastern European nation, who participates on a team of people who bring Nick to minister. He fills entire sports complexes in a country that has around one percent evangelical Christians, and God uses Nick to reach thousands, and display His glory.

Suffering Does Cooperate With God To Bring Good

We have begun to see some ways that God brings good from suffering. He seeks to get our attention, using suffering to bring us to Himself, bringing great temporal and eternal benefits. We have seen God using suffering to reveal Himself to us so that we know Him better, propelling us into a life of faith. Lastly, we have seen God revealing Himself in a way that is noticed by large numbers, who then recognize that He is God.

In the next chapter, we will explore how God uses suffering to forge a Christ-like character in us, and how He uses suffering to thrust us into effective ministry for Him.

CHAPTER NINE
Our Suffering Cooperates with God – (Part Two)

I mentioned in an earlier chapter that I struggled when I took my Greek class. I was not sure that I would pass the class. I became acquainted with two other students taking the same Greek class. We decided that we would study together. One of the students had taken a few weeks of Greek in a previous school. He knew enough to get us off the ground. Once the three of us were up to speed, we helped each other through the class. I can't speak for the other two, but I believe our cooperative effort may have gotten me through the class and into seminary.

In our last chapter, we talked about the fact that God works everything together for good. We discovered that "*all things God works for the good*" (Romans 8:28) means that all things cooperate with each other, causing our suffering to co-operate with God as He works in us and through us, just like the three Greek students cooperated. We discussed three ways that suffering works together with God to work good in our life. We saw that God sometimes uses suffering to get our attention, either to bring us to repentance or to keep us from going in a wrong direction. We also saw that God will use our suffering to bring us into a deeper relationship with Him, either by performing a miracle in our life that energizes our faith, or by undergirding us as we go through it. Lastly, we saw that God glorifies Himself by performing great miracles that have an impact upon a larger number of people, such as Elijah's confrontation of priests who "ministered" for false gods.

In this chapter, we will discuss two more ways that God uses suffering to bring about good.

God Uses Suffering To Develop Our Character

C.S. Lewis says, "The human spirit will not even begin to try to surrender self-will as long as all seems to be well with it."[lxviii] Lewis also says,

> ...but suppose that what you are up against is a surgeon whose intentions are wholly good. The kinder and more conscientious he is, the more inexorably he will go on cutting. If he yielded to your entreaties, if he stopped before the operation was complete, all the pain up to that point would have been useless...What do people mean when they say, "I am not afraid of God because I know He is good?" Have they never even been to a dentist?[lxix]

John Hick adds, "We have to recognize that the presence of pleasure and the absence of pain cannot be the supreme and overriding end for which the world exists. Rather, this world must be a   place of soul-making." (MINE: "character development").[lxx]

Suffering produces faith:

These quotes do not seem to agree with much of the theology of our day which states that believers should not have any suffering in their lives. As we saw in Chapter Three, we do experience suffering in our lives. What we did in Chapter Eight and now in Nine is to show how God leverages this suffering to produce good in our lives and those around us. Let us now explore the Scriptures to see how God uses our suffering, whether it be physical or emotional, to build our character. Paul, the Apostle says,

> *Not only so, but we also rejoice in our sufferings, because we know that suffering produces perseverance; perseverance, character; and character, hope* (Romans 5:3-4).

Paul tells us that we rejoice in sufferings. Again, a novel idea in our day.

Paul says that we rejoice in suffering. The word carries with it the unusual idea of boasting or glorying in the suffering.[lxxi] Paul tells his readers to have a deep inner rejoicing when experiencing suffering. He says that this rejoicing occurs because we know that God is going to do something in our walk with Him that will be to our benefit. If we benefit, then God will receive greater glory. Paul tells the Roman believers that God moves us through a progression which enables us to grow during suffering. Suffering, he says, produces patience. Patience is a "patient continuance (or waiting).[lxxii] Our waiting then produces character. Character is trustworthiness.[lxxiii] In other words, through suffering, God makes us a person that He can depend upon and others can depend upon. A person of character becomes a person of hope or faith.[lxxiv] In other words, when we have worked through this progression, we become someone who expects that God will do a work, either now or sometime in our future.

David demonstrates this. In Psalms 27, he talks about how many enemies are seeking to do him harm. It must have seemed like it was everyone, with some of them being very close to him, because he exclaims that even if his mother and father rejected him, he knows the Lord would take him in. He is declaring that if it got so bad that his parents rejected him, God would work in his life. As the Psalm comes to an end, he says, *"I will see the goodness of the LORD in the land of the living"* (Psalms 27:13). David had hope. Even though things looked bleak and many people wanted to do him harm, he maintained his belief that God would do something good.

The hope that is produced through suffering is a faith in the Lord. We have already talked about our ultimate hope in the Lord when we talked about the life we will have in eternity in Chapter Six. Getting back to Romans 5, I believe Paul (as with David in Psalms 27) was talking about hope for what God may do, while we live in the land of the living.

You may rightly remind us that sometimes people die in their suffering. Steve Saint is the son of Nate Saint, who was murdered by the natives that he and four others had hoped to reach for Christ. Steve, himself, became a missionary serving with Missionary Aviation Fellowship. In 1986, he was in Timbuktu. While waiting for his next assignment, he decided that he would like to drive around, even though he was told that it was too dangerous, but he couldn't find a vehicle that was in running condition. During this time, Steve was questioning whether his father's death had been necessary.

When he could not hire a vehicle, he asked someone to point him to a church. He met a pastor named Nouh Af Infa Yatara. Steve asked him how he came to faith. Nouh told him, and then said that when he became a believer, his mother tried to poison him, but he did not get sick or die. Steve eventually asked Nouh where he got his courage. He said the missionary gave him books about missionaries. He said the one that touched him most was about five missionaries who had been killed by stone age people in South America. Steve was stunned because it was the story of his father and the other four men who died!

Although Nate Saint's suffering had killed him, thousands of miles away, across the Atlantic ocean, God did a work in the life of a man "in the land of the living."[lxxv]

I added this story to remind us that good can even come in the land of the living, even if our suffering takes us home to our final reward. In our passage in Romans 5, Paul talks about developing a faith that gives the hope that we will see God work while we are still here on earth.

The process develops that kind of faith in us because as we move from one phase to the next in the progression, we are already seeing God do a work in us, which produces the hope that we will see Him do even more. When God develops faith/

hope in us, He is giving us a key ingredient to seeing God work in and through us. Faith is necessary to fulfilling God's plan for our life. The writer of Hebrews tells us, *"And without faith it is impossible to please God, because anyone who comes to him must believe that he exists and that he rewards those who earnestly seek him"* (Hebrews 11:6).

God's plan for us is bigger than we are, and bigger than we can imagine. We need to trust the Lord to do things that we cannot do on our own. If we are to keep plowing and finish the will of God in our life, we will need to get out of our comfort zone. So, as we see God do even little things in our character, we see that He can do even more in and through us, and so we grow into greater and greater faith.

Personally, I believe that I could have been content to stay in one place my whole life, but God has taken me on over 30 short-term mission trips in Africa, Asia, Central America and Europe. If you are reading this book, it means that it got published by some means. I got a D in my first college English course, which was a writing course. The courage and faith to do this came in bite sized chunks. As we see God do one thing, we believe Him for more. Part of His training is to develop faith through suffering. So, we have seen that God uses suffering to develop the kind of faith that will enable us to trust Him for amazing things that will bring glory to Him.

He also uses suffering to bring us to maturity.

The Apostle James also talks about the spiritual benefits of suffering. He tells us,

> *Consider it pure joy, my brothers, whenever you face trials of many kinds, because you know that the testing of your faith develops perseverance. Perseverance must finish its work so that you may be mature and complete, not lacking anything* (James 1:2-4).

James tells us that we should consider suffering a joy. We rejoice, not because we love the suffering, but because God is working in our lives. Both Paul and James encourage us to anticipate that God is producing character and maturity in us through our suffering. They are not encouraging us to have some sadistic pleasure in pain, but rather to look forward to the new thing that God is going to do in our life, as a result of how He is taking us through this season.

Randy Alcorn asks the question that if something as horrible as cancer makes us more like Christ, could we conclude that it is good? He tells about a friend who lost her husband to cancer. She said:

> ...his (God's) definition of good is different than mine. My 'good' would never include cancer and young widowhood. My 'good' would include healing and dying together in our sleep when we are in our nineties. But cancer was good because of what God did that He couldn't do any other way. Cancer was, in fact, necessary to make Bob and me look more like Jesus. So in love, God allowed what was best for us...in light of eternity.[lxxvi]

James also describes a process that God takes us through. We will get to the point. He says that suffering brings us to spiritual maturity. The word "mature," used by James, means "of full age."[lxxvii] None of us want to remain children in our walk with God. God does not desire that either, and He has designed a plan to help us become an adult. That plan involves suffering. James tells us that when we become mature, we will lack nothing.

Let's discuss some of the things that God supplies to the mature so that they "lack nothing." In a previous chapter, we discussed the wisdom that comes from the Holy Spirit (1 Corinthians 2). In verse six of that chapter, Paul says,

We do, however, speak a message of wisdom among the mature, but not the wisdom of this age or of the rulers of this age, who are coming to nothing (1 Corinthians 2:6).

Paul implies that if we do not become mature (if we have not grown up spiritually) we will not be able to handle this wisdom that comes from God. If we do not have the Kingdom wisdom of God, we are left with the wisdom of the world. Therefore, if we are an immature believer, we will need to rely upon the wisdom of the world as we make decisions, because God cannot entrust us with Kingdom wisdom. One aspect of this Kingdom wisdom, imparted by the Holy Spirit, is that we may need to go through suffering in order to become people who fulfill the will of God, even in difficult circumstances.

The writer of Hebrews concurs, saying,

Anyone who lives on milk, being still an infant, is not acquainted with the teaching about righteousness. But solid food is for the mature, who by constant use have trained themselves to distinguish good from evil (Hebrews 5:13-14).

If we are not mature, we will receive the kind of nourishment that children receive from their mothers. They will not be familiar with teaching about righteousness. The spiritually immature will not walk in righteousness, because they will not hear the wisdom that comes from the Holy Spirit and they will not truly understand the Word of God as they ought. If we are not mature, we will not understand or walk in righteousness in a way that fulfills the will of God in our life.

Paul expands upon this when he says,

"until we all reach unity in the faith and in the knowledge of the Son of God and become mature, attaining to the whole measure of the fullness of Christ" (Ephesians 4:13).

The context of this verse tells us that God has raised up spiritual leaders to prepare God's people to serve. As believers serve one another, using their spiritual gifts and ministering by the power of the Holy Spirit, they assist each other to become mature, that is, attaining to the full measure of Christ. We must allow God to bring us to maturity if we desire to be like Jesus. According to James, suffering is part of the maturing process.

Paul tells us one more thing about the mature, those who have grown up spiritually. He says,

"I press on toward the goal to win the prize for which God has called me heavenward in Christ Jesus. All of us who are mature should take such a view of things. And if on some point you think differently, that too God will make clear to you" (Philippians 3:14-15).

In talking about the fullness of Christ, Paul tells his readers that he has not arrived, but he says that he is pressing toward that prize. You can almost see Paul as a runner pressing toward the finish line, stretching to be the first to get there. Paul says that everyone who is mature should have this attitude. He says, "No one can really call themselves mature in Christ if they are not going for all that God has for them, with everything they have, no matter the cost." These are the people who will keep plowing. These are the people that will fulfill the plan that God has for them. Once again, we only become mature as we go through suffering.

We have seen a number of ways that God works for our good in suffering. As we consider the benefits that come with suffering, including 1) God getting our attention to keep us on track; 2) God revealing Himself to us by performing miracles or strengthening us in the middle of a battle; and 3) God bringing us to maturity so we can walk in the wisdom of the Holy Spirit, producing righteousness and giving us a zeal to go for everything that God has for us -- we will also be developing an inner rejoicing because we have come to realize that God is working good in the middle of our suffering.

Before we leave this chapter, we have one more way in which our suffering cooperates with God to bring good.

God Uses Suffering To Produce Effective Ministry

A great deal of Paul's ministry happened while he was suffering, or as a direct result of suffering. In Acts 16, Paul goes to Philippi, based upon a vision he received from the Lord. When he got there, a demon-possessed fortune teller kept following him, making life miserable. When Paul cast the demon out of the girl, he got thrown into prison because those who made money from the girl's predictions had lost their source of income.

While Paul and his sidekick, Silas were in prison, an earthquake occurred, opening all the cell doors. Miraculously, not one prisoner escaped. The jailer was ready to kill himself because he believed he had failed to do his job of securing the prisoners, but he realized that God had performed a miracle in keeping them from escaping, so he asked Paul and Silas what he had to do to be saved.

On another occasion, Paul was imprisoned again when the Jewish leaders falsely accused him of taking Greeks into the temple area.[lxxviii] Paul then traveled from city to city, either appealing his case or being protected from those who desired to kill him. In spite of this, Paul never stopped ministering. Twice he gave his testimony to large but hostile crowds (Acts 22 and 26), and he talked about the Lord in each of the courts that he was dragged into. Finally, when imprisoned in Rome, he praised God because the whole palace guard had heard about Christ, knowing that he had been imprisoned for the sake of Christ (Philippians 1:13).

A friend of mine recently went home to be with the Lord, after a brave battle with cancer. The staff at the doctor's office where she received chemo told her that she lit up the room, in spite of her own situation. She displayed joy and had a great impact on others, in spite of her own suffering.

Her story explains a key verse on ministry and suffering. Paul told the church in Corinth,

> *Praise be to the God and Father of our Lord Jesus Christ, the Father of compassion and the God of all comfort, who comforts us in all our troubles, so that we can comfort those in any trouble with the comfort we ourselves have received from God* (2 Corinthians 1:3-4).

It seems that when God comforts us in our troubles, it gives us the ability to minister to others.

I told you in the last chapter that I squeezed a three-year seminary program into three and a half years. Right before my last full year of seminary, the pastor who hired me left to plant a church in a nearby city. As the governing board of the church prayed about who to hire as the next pastor, they determined that I had not done an effective enough job of leading the youth ministry of the church, and decided that they wanted to allow the new pastor the option to choose the new youth pastor.

This decision seemed quite logical, unless you were me. I reasoned that I only had one more year of seminary to go. Was I so bad that they could not put up with me for one more year?[lxxix] I was hurting, experiencing all kinds of emotions. I certainly did not want to continue with those hurt feelings and the anger that I was feeling. The next day, when I went to attend my classes, I told a student who was a good friend. When he looked at me, I knew that he knew. He told me the same thing had just happened to him. Although he did not have answers at the time, it was cathartic just knowing that someone I respected had experienced the same thing.

Although telling my friend helped, I still struggled. I went to the district office of our denomination to talk with the District Superintendent. He was not there. However, the assistant District Superintendent was there. I explained to him what had happened. I told him the church told us we could live in their second parsonage and attend a different church if we wanted to. He shared his story of being let go. It so happened that he had been fired by his first church. Of course, he and his young wife were reeling at the time it occurred. She was a very good pianist. They had remembered that the church's piano was in disrepair. It was an upright and needed to be stripped and varnished. In order to avoid becoming bitter, they went back to the church and stripped and stained the piano as a gift. Wow! That spoke to me! We decided to remain in the church that had fired us and volunteer in a ministry where I was better suited. It helped us to work through attitudes towards those who had terminated us, and perhaps prevented me from giving root to bitterness.

The Holy Spirit ministers to us when we come across someone who is or has suffered in a way that is similar to our pain. It is especially true if the person who tells us that they suffered the same heartbreak as we have endured has made progress in gaining victory, or if they have come out on the other side. First of all, when we are cared for by someone who knows what we are experiencing, we no longer think that we are the only one. Secondly, if they have made progress, we have hope that we can move ahead, and we may learn some further tips that we can take from them.

Randy Alcorn tells of a woman who wrote to him. She tells him that she was sexually assaulted repeatedly by some neighborhood boys. In addition, her home life was chaotic -- full of drugs, dealing, and unsafe, neglectful parents. She shared her story with a mom and two adopted girls. They had experienced a similar home life. When one girl asked why God had allowed this woman to go through all of these things, the older sister said, "God allowed it so that she could understand and help us." The woman wept when she heard this. She realized that this happened to her so she could help others.[lxxx]

Seek The Lord

As we close this chapter, I want to ask you to take some time to reflect on the two major principles in this chapter.

1. *Are you going through suffering in your life?* If you haven't done so, ask the Lord the following:

- Is there some sin that I need to repent of? If so, ask God to forgive you for that sin and tell Him that, with His help, you will not do it again (repentance.)

- If there is not a specific sin, ask Him if there are areas of your life that He would like to change so that you can move to greater degrees of maturity.

2. *Have you gone through something, or are you currently going through something that could be of help to others?* You may say, "I am not sufficiently healed in this area. My wife has come a long way in her painful relational situation, but still experiences some tough days, but God has used her to be a real encouragement to many others who have experienced similar pain and in so doing, she is blessed!"

You may have actually been asking God to reveal to you some area of ministry in your life. Perhaps, God is showing you that your place of greatest pain is to be your place of greatest ministry. Author and speaker Lance Wallnau, says, "Show me your pain, show me your passion and I will show you your purpose."[lxxxi]

Can you see why both Paul and James tell us to rejoice? God uses painful experiences to make us Christ-like, and to help others become more Christ-like, as well.

As we continue to learn principles that will help us make our way through suffering, we found out that we can endure more easily because we have a glorious eternity waiting for us. We know that the Holy Spirit, along with Jesus, is praying for us as we go through difficulty, because God uses suffering to co-operate with Him to achieve His Kingdom purposes.

In the next couple of chapters, we will discover some

benefits that God has provided for us to enable us to walk through difficulty.

CHAPTER TEN

God Has Spared Nothing

While on vacation in Florida, Gareth Griffith, a management consultant in London, decided to try sky diving. He was jumping in tandem with Michael Costello, an experienced instructor. Something went wrong. The main chute failed to open. No big deal, they had a back up chute. The backup failed also. The two men went into a violent spin as they plummeted to their destiny. The instructor corrected the spin and regained control of the fall. Griffith was on the bottom and the instructor was on top. As they neared the ground, the instructor folded his arms and legs, causing the pair to rotate. In doing so, the instructor hit the ground first, cushioning his student's blow. Griffith survived. Costello wasn't so fortunate—he sacrificed his own life so that Griffith could live.[lxxxii] He did not spare his own life.

We look at the above story and are amazed by the sacrifice. We wonder if we would do the same if faced with a similar situation. Paul tells us that there are rare occasions when someone will do what Michael Costello did. Paul, however, tells us that God did the same for us when we were sinners, people separated from God and in rebellion to Him. Paul says,

> *Very rarely will anyone die for a righteous man, though for a good man someone might possibly dare to die. But God demonstrates his own love for us in this: While we were still sinners, Christ died for us* (Romans 5:7-8).

Paul picks up this theme again as he tells us about the

ways that God helps us to keep plowing when we go through suffering and trouble. He says,

He who did not spare his own Son, but gave him up for us all--how will he not also, along with him, graciously give us all things (Romans 8:32)?

Have you ever seen something in a store that you wanted to purchase until you saw the price tag? You decided that maybe you don't need it as bad as you thought. God looked at humanity and said, "I really want them to know Me! I want to have a relationship them! As He considered how He could take care of the sin issue and still remain just, He saw the price tag. The only way He could redeem humans was to send His Only Perfect Son to live on earth and take the punishment for everyone's sins by dying a horrific death on a Roman cross. We are told that God did not abstain[lxxxiii] from paying the full price of His Son. Everyone who has received Jesus Christ into his or her life has benefited from the incredible sacrifice that God made to purchase our salvation.

Paul then draws a logical conclusion. He says that if God did not hold back that which is most precious to Him, won't He also give us everything else that we need in order to fully live the life that Jesus died to purchase for us?

Peter concurs, saying:

His divine power has given us everything we need for life and godliness through our knowledge of him who called us by his own glory and goodness. Through these he has given us his very great and precious promises, so that through them you may participate in the divine nature and escape the corruption in the world caused by evil desires (2 Peter 1:3-4).

Peter says that God has given those who know Him everything they need. The provisions that God has provided are given to us in God's precious promises. These promises are found in God's Word, the Bible.

In the next three chapters, we are going to take a look at some of the promises God has made to us, so that we may take advantage of them and fulfill God's will for our life, even when we suffer. All of them are very important, so there is not a priority order. Each will be important to us at any given time.

God Forgives Those Who Trust In Him/He Enables The Forgiven To Forgive Others

When Adam and Eve sinned, their relationship with God was severed. Paul tells us that *"the wages of sin is death"* (Romans 6:23). Although the death talked about here includes physical death, the primary death spoken of here is spiritual death, separation from God. We have talked previously about our severed relationship with God which dooms us to make decisions without His guidance. Unfortunately, when Adam and Eve sinned, they passed spiritual death to their children and to all mankind. Paul tells us, *"Therefore, just as sin entered the world through one man, and death through sin, and in this way death came to all men, because all sinned..."* (Romans 5:12). This explains why our world is in such a mess. Humans have made decisions without God's input for millennia, which have taken us further from truth and God.

God sent Jesus to solve that problem. He died to pay the penalty for our sin. *"For Christ died for sins once for all, the righteous for the unrighteous, to bring you to God"* (1 Peter 3:18).

By paying the penalty for our sin, Jesus demolished the wall of sin that stood between humans and God. He took the punishment for all the sins of every human who ever lived and who would ever live. The penalty has been paid, and God offers forgiveness and a new relationship with Himself to all who receive Christ by faith. Everyone who asks Christ to come into their life, to forgive them of their sins and become the Lord of their life receives forgiveness for all their sins -- every sinful thought, word, or action. There is no way that we can calculate the size and depth of our sins. He has forgiven us of them all.

The Psalmist tells us that God removes our sins from us *as far as the east is from the west* (Psalms 103:12). The east and west never meet. Our sins are gone. Sin no longer stands in the way of our relationship with God. Once our relationship with God is restored, we can begin to get to know Him and it is only then that we can begin to hear and understand His wisdom. It is only then that we can begin to experience the peace, joy and purpose that God has for us. It is then that we begin to know what life is really all about. It is then that we are fully alive.

A key goal of this new life is to become like Jesus. As Jesus hung on the cross, He said, *"Father forgive them, for they do not know what they are doing"* (Luke 23:34).

Later, in the Book of Acts, we see Stephen expressing forgiveness to those who were stoning Him to death. He said, *"Lord, do not hold this sin against them"* (Acts 7:60). God also wants us to forgive those who have sinned against us.

In Matthew 6, Jesus gives His disciples a model prayer to assist them in praying for God's Kingdom to come to the earth. In the middle of that prayer, He tells them to pray, *"Forgive us our debts, as we also have forgiven our debtors"* (Matthew 6:12). Jesus teaches them to ask God to forgive them in the same way they have forgiven others. If we have not forgiven, then those who pray this are telling God He does not need to forgive them. Just in case the disciples have missed this point, He later tells them:

> *For if you forgive men when they sin against you, your heavenly Father will also forgive you. But if you do not forgive men their sins, your Father will not forgive your sins* (Matthew 6:14-15).

Jesus tells them plainly that God will not forgive us if we do not forgive (see also Colossians 3:13).

Later on, in Matthew's Gospel, we find Jesus illustrating this point. As the disciples are listening to Jesus teach, Peter asks how many times he needs to forgive someone. He feels like He is generous with seven. Jesus says, "No, not seven times, but seventy-seven times".[lxxxiv] He then tells a parable of a man who owed a king so much he could never hope to pay him back. The man pleads for mercy and the king forgives the entire debt. Then, the man who had been forgiven the debt came across a man who owed him a small debt. He would not forgive the man his small debt. Others went to the king and told him what had happened, and the king put the first man in prison until he could pay the debt. Jesus said, *"This is how my heavenly Father will treat each of you unless you forgive your brother from your heart"* (Matthew 18:35).

Again, God tells us that He will not forgive us if we do not forgive. We are the man who had a debt he couldn't pay. Our sins were, and are, that great. We should then be willing to forgive those whose sin against us is small by comparison.

Let me tell you about our friend Mary.[lxxxv] Mary's mother had been killed by a terrorist group when she was twelve years old. This obviously had a terrible impact on her. Although, she came from a nominal Christian home, she received Christ at age eighteen. Sometime after that, she began to receive discipleship training from a missionary from Europe. We were in her country, teaching our *Breaking Free* Course.[lxxxvi] The missionary called her and asked her to come. She said, "I can't. I am not feeling well." He said, "It is the devil. You must come." She made the long trip by herself. When she got there, she sat outside the room where my wife was teaching about forgiveness, with time given for each of privately deal with unforgiveness.

At the end of the seminar, a time was designated for people to share testimonies. Mary went forward and told how she had forgiven the men who had killed her mother. During that week, she felt the Lord call her to engage in ministry that would help others gain freedom in their lives. She now receives invitations from all over her country asking her to come and minister to people. She helps many deal with forgiveness and emotional issues. It began as she was given the grace to forgive.

We may wonder why God wants us to forgive those who have sinned against us, sometimes in heinous ways. In addition, you may wonder why we are talking about this in a section on God's provision for us.

There are three key reasons that God wants us to forgive:

1. As we have ministered our *Breaking Free* course around the world, we have found that *unwillingness to forgive is the number one reason believers do not gain freedom.*

2. Secondly, *when we forgive, we are like God.*

3. Thirdly, *those who do not forgive can become bitter.* The writer of Hebrews tells us that bitterness becomes like a root that defiles us (Hebrews 12:15). When a person is bitter toward another person, the bitter person sees everything the person toward whom they are bitter through dark glasses. Their whole attitude toward them is tainted and loveless. In Ephesians 4:31, Paul tells the Ephesians to get rid of all bitterness. The word here describes bitterness as poison.[lxxxvii] Bitterness slowly kills the person who is bitter (at least emotionally) and others who must be around them. When we are bitter, we negatively impact others as well.

We went to a place in India that seemed like the end of the world. There was a small group of people waiting at an elder's house for us to share the Word of God. Afterwards, our interpreter asked those who had serious needs to come for prayer. Everyone for whom we prayed was healed by the Lord (including a baby with a severe fever and was probably near death) except one. We came to the elders' wife, who had serious arthritis. My wife felt led to ask the woman if she had anyone she needed to forgive. She said, "I will never forgive them." It seems there was a border dispute and she felt wronged. On a night, when God was present to heal, she went home bitter, but without being healed.

On the other hand, we were ministering *Breaking Free* in a European nation. When we divided into groups of men and women for confession and prayer, a woman came to the chair in the middle of the room. We had noticed her before this meeting helping to care for details around the church. Her tousled hair covered much of her face and she wore a big frumpy sweatshirt. She shared her story. When she was eighteen years old, she went on a boat with some young men. They were drinking. Eventually they violated the woman in many ways, and threw her overboard into the very cold water to die. She wanted to die, but she lived.

It was now eighteen years later. She felt terrible about herself and had already had a failed marriage. As she shared her story, she said that, that night she wanted to forgive the men who had violated her and left her for dead. My wife led her in a prayer to forgive these men, and then to ask God to bless them. As you can imagine, there were many tears and hugs.

We took a break, and the woman went home. When she came back, she had pulled her hair her back and was wearing a beautiful white blouse, something she had not done in eighteen years. We hardly even recognized her. When the meeting was over, she began to laugh, and we all joined in. Eighteen years of laughter bubbled out in that amazing moment!

If you have someone you have not forgiven, you will not live as fully as God desires, and you may not be able to keep plowing when you go through hardship.

I want you to put the book down and ask God if there is anyone you have not forgiven. Ask Him to help you. Pray this prayer:

> *"Father, I thank you that you have forgiven me.*
>
> *Now I want to forgive* __________ (specifically name those who have wronged you)
>
> *for* __________ (be specific about what you are forgiving them for).

Now Father, I ask you to forgive them and I ask you to bless them. (Name some ways that they need to be blessed)."

If it is appropriate, you may want to tell them you have forgiven them. If they did not know you held bitterness against them, you can confess to God alone. Although it would be wonderful if the person asks you to forgive them, you do not need to wait for them to ask. You can, and for your sake you should, forgive them -- even if they do not ask. Forgiving those who have offended or hurt us will give us freedom.

God has forgiven us of all our sin. He gives us the ability to forgive others. This will help us to live fully for God. Failing to forgive others may actually be the reason for some of our problems. God may use difficulties to get our attention so that we do forgive, or we may be miserable because we are a bitter person.

We are now going to look at a second provision God has given to us, to assist us to live for Him and to also assist us as we navigate through hardship.

God Has Sent The Holy Spirit To Assist Us
To Keep Plowing And Fulfill His Plan

On the night Jesus' trial began, Peter boldly declared that he would never betray Jesus in any way, even if it meant that he would die with Jesus. As we know, Peter denied that he even knew Jesus three times that night. Jesus had already said to Peter that *"the spirit is willing, but the body is weak"* (Matthew 26:41). In other words, in the natural, we are weak and may crumble. This is why Jesus told His disciples to wait for what the Father had promised (Luke 24:49). The Father had promised that He would send the Holy Spirit to assist them in their ministry.

We have already discussed a number of ways that the Holy Spirit assists us in fulfilling the purpose God has for us. I will mention them again, along with some other benefits the

Holy Spirit brings. (It is not a problem to mention them again because they are extremely important).

He gives us life.

During Jesus' conversation with Nicodemus, Jesus told him that he (and we) must be born of the Spirit if we are going to have the life God offers (John 3:5). The reason that Adam and Eve became separate from God was because when they sinned, wanting to determine right and wrong without God, the Holy Spirit withdrew from their human spirit and they became spiritually dead. When people receive Jesus Christ into their lives, the Holy Spirit comes to dwell in their human spirit, and they become fully alive -- spirit, soul, and body. The Holy Spirit then infuses believers with the very life of God. This is why Paul says, *"if anyone does not have the Spirit of Christ, he does not belong to Christ"* (Romans 8:9). When we receive Jesus, we are born of the Spirit.

He gives us Kingdom wisdom.

We have already discussed 1 Corinthians 2. This passage tells us that the Spirit knows the mind of God, so He is the one who can tell us what is on the heart of God. When we are faced with a situation where we do not know what to do, the Holy Spirit can give us God's wisdom for the situation. We need God's wisdom at all times. We want to hear His perspective so we will engage in the activities that will bear the most fruit for His Kingdom.

We especially need God's wisdom when we are experiencing some type of suffering, rejection, or persecution. The Holy Spirit may give us insight concerning where the hardship is coming from: Is it an attack of the enemy? Is it from human origin or from the corrupted creation? Although we may never learn the source of our pain, we will want to know what God wants us to learn in the situation: Is He building character?

Does He want us to exercise spiritual authority? Does He want to perform some type of miracle, such as a healing? The Holy Spirit will reveal this to us if we ask.

For instance, Job learned why he had suffered, but not until the end of the Book of Job. My wife and I pastored a church from 1989 to 1998. Leading the church presented many challenges. The last few years were particularly difficult. I believed, and still do, that a great deal of the resistance to what we were led to do was an attack from the enemy. However, as I have looked back over those years, although I learned much, I wish I had been more diligent in asking God what He wanted to teach me during those years. If we seek the Holy Spirit about all those things, He will answer us, speaking to us directly, often through the Scriptures.

Of course, there are times when He may not tell us where the pain comes from or specifically what He wants to do in the situation, because we will only learn what we are supposed to learn by going through it.

He makes us like Jesus.

Jesus lived a perfect life while He lived on earth. We are told that He did not sin (Hebrews 4:15). This means that He did not have one character flaw. He did not have one immoral thought or action, and He obeyed His Father, fulfilling everything the Father had sent Him to do. One of the Holy Spirit's ministries is to work in our life and make us more like Jesus.

> *"But the fruit of the Spirit is love, joy, peace, patience, kindness, goodness, faithfulness, gentleness and self-control. Against such things there is no law"* (Galatians 5:22-23).

A fruit tree produces fruit when it is healthy. The Holy Spirit is totally healthy. Therefore, when we follow His lead, He will produce this fruit in us. It is the very character of Jesus. When we start to become like Jesus, we walk in peace and joy, and we will manifest love. As we continue this growth process, we will become increasingly more like Jesus and if we are like Jesus, we will live for others like He did. When that is the case, we will fulfill His will for us and keep plowing, even when things get tough.

As Paul nears the end of his letter to the Romans, he prays:

May the God of hope fill you with all joy and peace as you trust in him, so that you may overflow with hope by the power of the Holy Spirit" (Romans 15:13).

The indication here is that as we develop the character of Jesus, we will overflow with hope. Even in difficulty we will look with anticipation to our future on earth and in eternity. Even in the middle of difficulty we will know that God is working, giving us much to look forward to. We will have that attitude that Jesus had when, as Isaiah prophesied, *"After the suffering of his soul, he will see the light of life and be satisfied"* (Isaiah 53:11). As Jesus considered His suffering, He saw what the Father would do in bringing billions to Himself. As a result, He was satisfied. As we develop the character of Jesus, we can look at the things we go through and be satisfied that God has done a work in and through us.

He has inspired and will illuminate the Word of God.

The Holy Spirit moved upon the Scripture writers in such a way that they wrote what He wanted them to write, even though each book reflects the personality of the human author:

Above all, you must understand that no prophecy of Scripture came about by the prophet's own interpretation. For prophecy never had its origin in the will of man, but men spoke from God as they were carried along by the Holy Spirit (2 Peter 1:20-21).

The Holy Spirit carried along, or drove,[lxxxviii] the writers to write what they wrote. This means that the Scriptures are the divinely inspired Word of God. Paul agrees in 2 Timothy

3:16-17. Paul emphasizes that all Scripture is inspired by God. We can depend upon the Bible. The Bible is the only book we can read and know for sure that we are getting truth. The Holy Spirit is the author of the Bible.

When I was in seminary, we read a classic piece of literature. Many people expressed what they thought it meant. Later, the author, who was still alive, shared the meaning of the piece. The experts were all wrong. It helped to have the author tell us what he wanted to communicate. The Holy Spirit inspired the Bible, and He is still alive. As we read and study, He will highlight truths to us showing us the meaning of the Scripture and how it applies to us or a group that we are part of.

Jeremiah prophesied during the reigns of several kings. He sought to call the Southern Kingdom of Israel (Judah) to repentance. They would not repent, so Jeremiah told the residents of Judah that they would be taken into captivity in another land for seventy years (Jeremiah 25:11). Seventy years later, the Holy Spirit illuminated that Scripture to Daniel, who was in captivity. He began to pray that the people of Judah would be able to go back to their country (Daniel 9:2). God answered that prayer. It was the Holy Spirit who highlighted that passage and inspired Daniel to pray.

The Holy Spirit will do that for us, as well. I have had several occasions when the Holy Spirit has highlighted a Scripture to me. When my wife and I were praying about getting married, God gave both of us Psalms 37:4-5 without the other knowing. We sensed in our heart that this was from God. It has been shown to be correct for nearly 43 years.

The Holy Spirit empowers us for ministry

We have already talked about the need to minister in the power of the Holy Spirit. Jesus' earthly disciples had been prepared better than any other disciples in history. They had been students of Rabbi Jesus. They had heard Him teach and they saw Him perform many miracles such as healings, raising people from the dead, and exercising authority over nature. They knew that He had been executed, and yet they saw Him several times after the resurrection. How could anyone be better prepared for ministry? Yet Jesus told them to wait until they had been empowered by the Holy Spirit. He knew that if they had not been empowered by the Spirit, they would succumb to their human weakness, and fail to fulfill His will.

Let's look at four ways that the Holy Spirit empowers us for ministry:

1. *He gives boldness and anointing.*

After praying for ten days, the Holy Spirit came upon the Early Church and empowered them for ministry. They went into the crowd and Peter boldly preached the Word of God. His words were so powerful that the people asked Him what they needed to do to be saved. (See Acts Chapter 2 and Acts 4:24-37, to see two examples of The Holy Spirit giving boldness).

2. *He helps us to evangelize.*

On the night that Jesus' trial began, He told the disciples that when the Holy Spirit comes, *"He will convict the world of guilt in regard to sin and righteousness and judgment." (John 16:8).* In other words, He will give unbelievers a deep inner conviction that they need to be saved from sin. Jesus also told them that the Holy Spirit would talk about Jesus (John 15:26). This means that as we share our faith in Jesus, the Holy Spirit will be working in the life of the one we are speaking to.

I had a roommate at the time I met Kerry. He had come to a nearby town for work. He was out walking one day and saw that young people from a church had written some positive graffiti about Jesus. The Holy Spirit was working. When he saw those words, he concluded that if the kids thought that way about Jesus, Christianity might be real. This led to a series of events that brought him to Christ. The kids witness was graffiti. The Holy Spirit did the rest.

3. *He gives us gifts for ministry.*

We previously mentioned that God gives to each believer supernatural abilities for ministry. These abilities empower believers for ministries such as teaching, giving, administration and serving. They also give believer the ability to speak in other tongues, receive discernment from God, pray for healing, and others. He gives some leadership gifts. (See Romans 12:1-8; 1 Corinthians 12:7-11 and Ephesians 4:7-13).[lxxxix] As we observe the gifts that God gives to us (and our leaders confirm them), it helps us determine where God would have us minister.

4. *He guides us.*

If we are in need of direction, we can ask the Holy Spirit. I remember a time when Kerry and I went to a meeting in a house church in India. I believe I had been scheduled to speak. Our pastor friend, Sanjay, said, "I believe Kerry should speak because there are so many women and children." Kerry spoke and asked me if I had something. I had a few short words and felt like I was done, but the meeting was not. Pastor Sanjay got up and closed the meeting and about twelve people raised their hand to receive Jesus. God had led all three of us that night, and He received the glory. We especially need the Holy Spirit's direction when we are suffering, because we may tend to make unwise decisions in order to relieve the pain, at least temporarily. The Holy Spirit will always guide us when we seek His direction.

At the beginning of the chapter, we said that God gave His best, Jesus, to enable us to fulfill the plan He has for us. Because He has already given us the best, He will give us everything else we need to fulfill His plan. In this chapter, we talked about the fact that God forgives us of all our sins if we come to Him, confessing them. He also gives us the supernatural ability to forgive those who sin against us.

Then, we talked about how the Holy Spirit helps us in every aspect of our ministry. In the middle of the chapter, we challenged you to seek God for those that you need to forgive. If you have not done that yet, go back to the end of the section on forgiveness and work through that process, so that you don't wind up in bitterness.

As you complete that, ask the Holy Spirit to take control of your life and fill you up so that you can walk in His power for your personal life and ministry. Pray something like this:

"Father, I thank you that the Holy Spirit came into my life when I received Jesus. I now ask the Holy Spirit to fill me in every way for my life and ministry. Thank You that You promise to do this, according to Acts 1:8!"

In the next two chapters, we will talk about some of God's other provisions to assist us in our walk with Him, even when we are experiencing difficulty. It is so wonderful that God has provided so much for us!

CHAPTER ELEVEN
God Has Spared Nothing - Part 2

Paul and his team had very fruitful ministry in Ephesus. It was a city filled with sorcery and the need for deliverance ministry. So many who had practiced sorcery came to know the Lord that they burned their books of sorcery, valued at 50,000 drachmas.[xc] Later, we find Jewish men unsuccessfully engaging in the ministry of exorcism. Their attempts, however, indicated that many of the Ephesians lived in bondage. It was a place where the Church faced serious challenges.

As Paul wrote his letter to the Ephesian Church,[xci] he understood that God had indeed provided whatever they needed as Christians (Romans 8:32). As he prayed for them, he said:

I keep asking that the God of our Lord Jesus Christ, the glorious Father, may give you the Spirit of wisdom and revelation, so that you may know him better (Ephesians 1:17).

He went on to inform them of three key truths that they would need to understand in order to fulfill God's purpose in Ephesus and beyond.

Paul understood that it doesn't matter what benefits God provides for us to live for Him if we don't use them. If we don't use what God has provided for us, we are like someone who has millions of dollars in a bank account, and yet continues to make purchases and pay bills based upon a minimum wage job.

There could be two reasons why someone may not take

advantage of a large bank account. One reason may be that the person may have a "me do" mentality. In other words, he is acting like the toddler who has a parent or grandparent by their side as they try some new skill, but refuses help because he wants to do it himself, saying "me-do!" The other reason that someone may not take advantage of the large bank account is that they may not be aware that they have the money.

If either of these is true of us, we may be seeking to follow the Lord in good times and in times of suffering without the benefit of all that God had provided.

In Chapter Ten, we began to discuss some of the benefits that God has given to us in order to enable us to keep plowing in all circumstances. First, we said that God has forgiven us of all our sins and has given us the grace to forgive others. These gifts free us up to walk in a relationship with God and enable us to live a life that is not weighed down by bitterness. Secondly, we talked about the role the Holy Spirit plays in our life as we seek to follow Him. In this chapter, we will talk about two more provisions in the Kingdom-benefit package: The Word of God and Prayer. Although God speaks to us in many ways, prayer and seeking God in His Word are key to hearing from, and communicating with, the Lord.

The Word Of God

I have talked about the Word of God, the Bible, throughout the book. I believe firmly that we cannot be all that God wants us to be or do all that He wants us to do unless we actively seek to know Him, and as we seek to learn what life is all about, as revealed in Scripture.

In our discussion of the ministry of the Holy Spirit, we noted that God gave us the Bible, as the Holy Spirit inspired writers to write exactly what He wanted them to write. In other words, even though the personality of the writers emerges in each of the books of the Bible, each writer wrote exactly what the Holy Spirit told them to write. Therefore, the Bible contains the very words of God. Certainly, if our desire is to serve the Lord, we will want to hear what He has to say about life.

The Word of God is Truth

Humans have developed many philosophies, economic systems and religions in their quest for truth. However, we only need to look to the Word of God to find truth. Psalms 119 is the longest of the Psalms. It is almost exclusively about the Bible. The Psalmist says, *"All your words are true; all your righteous laws are eternal"* (Psalms 119:160). The Bible is eternal truth. Truth does not change. The Bible is the only place where we can be sure that we are getting complete truth! Jesus agrees with the Psalmist. As Jesus prays for His disciples before His trial, execution and ultimately His resurrection, He prays, "Sanctify them by the truth; your word is truth" (John 17:17).

The Word Sets Us Apart to Serve God

Jesus' prayed that the disciples would be sanctified in truth. The word *sanctify* is similar to the word *holy*. He is asking the Father to set these men apart for Him, and only Him, through the truth. The Bible tells us who God is, how we can relate to Him and how He wants us to live. When we are living according to God's truth, we are living as God wants us to live. When we live according to the truths of the Bible, we will reject the philosophies and religions of the world, because we will be living for the One True Eternal God!

Paul adds to this when he writes to his young protégé, Timothy.

> *All Scripture is God-breathed and is useful for teaching, rebuking, correcting, and training in righteousness, so that the man of God may be thoroughly equipped for every good work"* (2Timothy 3:16-17).

We have already discussed this verse, but it is important that we talk about it in this context. He tells us that the Scripture is good for teaching, the truth that God desires us to live by. The Word of God rebukes us, which means that it shows us when we have sinned or gone the wrong direction. It does not stop there, but also shows us how to get on track when we have erred in some way. It acts like a spiritual GPS. When I am going someplace that I have not been before, I use my GPS. Occasionally, I miss a turn. The GPS immediately begins to tell me what to do to get back on the right route. God's Word does the same.

The Word of God also trains us in righteous living. Paul concludes that when we get the Word of God into our lives and we allow it to guide and train us, we will be equipped for every work that God has for us.

The Word of God does more than just give us better information to assist us to make decisions. He says that the Word of God can transform us into another person. The word "transformed" means a metamorphosis. [xcii]

> *Do not conform any longer to the pattern of this world, but be transformed by the renewing of your mind. Then you will be able to test and approve what God's will is--his good, pleasing and perfect will* (Romans 12:2).

This metamorphosis happens as we renew, or renovate, our mind.[xciii]

The writer of Hebrews tells how the Word of God renews our mind.

> *For the word of God is living and active. Sharper than any double-edged sword, it penetrates even to dividing soul and spirit, joints and marrow; it judges the thoughts and attitudes of the heart* (Hebrews 4:12).

Dr. Ed Silvoso tells us that this means that the Word of God penetrates so deeply into our being that it exposes the arguments of our human reasoning as lies, and establishes the truth into our human spirit. [xciv] As a result, God uses the Word of God to show us truth, and to change the way that we think. We see things from God's point of view and, as a result, we live our lives the way He wants us to live them. We can facilitate God's changing of our mind by spending time, on a regular basis, getting the Word into our lives.

How to Get the Word of God into Your Life

About fifteen years ago, I went to my doctor for a routine appointment. He told me that my blood work showed that my blood sugar was too high. I went on a stricter diet, and the blood sugar came down but not sufficiently to avoid medication. We had prayed that God would do a miracle, but He choose not to do so. So the doctor prescribed medication. Shortly after, I began to get the medicine into my body, my blood sugar numbers were transformed. It has remained lower as long as I regularly take the medicine and am disciplined in my eating and exercise. If I choose not to take the medication, my blood sugar would go up to unhealthy levels.

It is the same with the Word of God. If we want our mind to change, then we must get a steady diet of the Word of God.

During my last year at university and the first couple of years after I graduated, I received training from the Navigators. They taught us to get the Word of God into our lives. They used a hand to show us five ways to get the Word of God into our life.[xcv] Here are the five ways:

Hear the Word of God (Romans 10:17)

We have many opportunities to hear the Word of God in church, Sunday School classes, small groups, and the internet. Let us learn from gifted teachers on a regular basis.

Read the Word of God (Revelation 1:3)

I recommend that you read the Bible every day, if possible. If you read two chapters from the Old Testament and one from the New Testament every day, you can read the entire Bible in thirteen months. You may want to make it a habit to read it through each year. There are many programs available to help you read the Bible in a year.

Study the Bible (Acts 17:11)

There are many helps to aide you in Bible study. Ask your pastor to help you choose one. I recommend that you get into a small group Bible Study. If you do, you will learn from each member in the group, and you will be developing a support base that will help you grow in the Lord, and provide a group that will help to meet each other's needs. I would love to go into more detail here concerning how you can study the Bible, but that is beyond the scope of this book.

Memorize the Word of God (Psalms 119:9,11)

As verses stand out to you in your reading or study, memorize them. You can also find organizations that have Scripture memory programs that will assist you to choose key Scriptures on basic topics.[xcvi]

Meditate upon the Word of God (Psalms 1:1-3)

We meditate upon the Word of God when we think about what we have heard, read, studied and memorized, while asking the Holy Spirit to show us how the passages relate to our lives. As we read, we may ask the Lord, "Is there something I need to repent of, or some new discipline You would like to add to my life?" We can ask many other questions. In this step, we are taking what we are learning and making it part of the way that we live. As God answers these questions, obey what He tells you in His Word.

We may look at this and think "This is going to require

a lot of me!" Doesn't anything that is worth doing take effort? We are talking about being effective in fulfilling God's plan for our life! We are talking about doing what God created us to do! We are talking about completing God's plan, even when we are going through suffering! Are we willing to pay a price in order to do that? If the answer is yes, you will find ways to daily (unless impossible) read the Bible, and regularly hear, study and memorize God's Word.

Prayer

I have heard a number of people say that they miss talking to a family member or friend after that person died. Unfortunately, when Adam and Eve decided that they wanted to be able to determine what is right and wrong on their own by eating from the Tree of the Knowledge of Good and Evil, they died spiritually. Because they died spiritually, they were no longer able to communicate with God, which has resulted in the problems we see in the world today.

God wanted, and still wants, to have a relationship with every man, woman, girl, and boy. He sent Jesus to die for our sins, those things that create the barrier that exists between us and God:

> *For Christ died for sins once for all, the righteous for the unrighteous, to bring you to God* (1 Peter 3:18).

When we receive Jesus as our Lord and Savior, we reconnect with God, and have the great privilege of communing with (talking with and listening to) Him. We call this prayer.

Prayer is Not a Letter to Santa Claus

Therefore I tell you, whatever you ask for in prayer, believe that you have received it, and it will be yours" (Mark 11:24).

We sometimes read Scriptures like this quote from Jesus, and look at prayer like it is a letter to Santa Claus, a wish list of all of our wants. Certainly God does answer many of those prayers because He is a loving, heavenly Father. Just this morning, my wife and I went out for our daily walk which is also our time of praying together. It looked like it was going to rain and so we asked the Lord to hold off the rain until we got back. He did! Not long after we got into our house, it began to rain really hard. So, we can ask God for anything, but I believe that God wants us to make the things that will advance His Kingdom in our life and in the world our priority in prayer.

We get a glimpse of that in Luke 11. The disciples observed Jesus praying and asked Him to teach them to pray (Luke 11:1). Jesus then gave them what we call "The Lord's Prayer". It is actually a model prayer. He gave them five areas where they (and we) are to pray:

Father, hallowed be your name...

Jesus says that we are to acknowledge that we are coming into the presence of our Father. When we came to Jesus, we became part of His family. Certainly, the fact that He is our Father shows the closeness we have with Him and will stimulate our faith. When He says, "hallowed be your name," He is encouraging us to worship God. God is holy! There is none like Him! As we get to know Him and His character, we will find many things for which we can worship Him. He is eternal and infinite! He is righteous and full of love! He is just and He is merciful, and so much more! He is worthy!

But I believe that this is also a prayer that His Name would be hallowed throughout the earth. He is Creator! He is God! He is worthy! He deserves to be worshipped   throughout the earth. Therefore, we are praying that God would be "hallowed" among all the   peoples of the earth.

Your kingdom come...

Although God is creator, the first humans and everyone since, have rebelled against God. The creation has also been corrupted. As we pray for His Kingdom to come, we are praying that individuals will become followers of Christ and spread the Kingdom of God to every part of the earth, so that He can receive the glory due Him from every part of our planet.

Give us each day our daily bread...

God promises to meet our needs. We are to pray for those things that we need in order to live and do His will. We are praying for food and shelter. This probably means that we need a job. If we don't have one, we should pray that God gives us one. Not only does God meet our personal and family needs, He also meets the needs for the ministries that we are involved in. I will be sharing some examples of how God meets needs when I talk about Him providing for our every need, in the next chapter.

Forgive us our sins, for we also forgive everyone who sins against us...

We spent a great deal of time talking about this in the last chapter. If you have questions, go back and read Chapter Ten.

And lead us not into temptation...

James tells us that God does not tempt us, but rather we are carried away by our own desires (James 1:13). Therefore, it is not God who does the tempting. Matthew's version of the Lord's Prayer gives some insight. *"And lead us not into temptation, but deliver us from the evil one"* (Matthew 6:13). You will notice that he adds "deliver us from the evil one." This indicates that temptation comes from the enemy, in the areas where we may have unholy desires. Therefore, our prayer should be that God would assist us, so we don't succumb to the enemy's temptations.

You will notice that these are Kingdom-focused prayers. It does talk about daily bread and overcoming temptation, but in asking for our daily bread, we are not asking for large amounts of what we want. Rather, we are asking for what we need. In asking to overcome temptation, we are asking God to help us to continue to live righteously. When we do, we will live in a way that properly represents Jesus. In addition, when we live the right way, the way God wants us to, we will also live to serve others.

Up to this point, I have been talking about the general areas that we can pray about. Prayer is asking God to do what He wants to do on earth. It doesn't preclude us asking for special favors. He does them in many cases, but as a believer, our heart should be to see the will of God accomplished on the earth and in our life.

I now want to take a look at some Scriptures that discuss prayer during times of hardship. The Philippian' church experienced both persecution and poverty. Because of that, we know their life was difficult. Paul gave them some advice for their time of difficulty. He told them:

Rejoice in the Lord always. I will say it again: Rejoice! Let your gentleness be evident to all. The Lord is near. Do not be anxious about anything, but in everything, by prayer and petition, with thanksgiving, present your requests to God. And the peace of God, which transcends all understanding, will guard your hearts and your minds in Christ Jesus (Philippians 4:4-7).

First of all, Paul tells them to rejoice. This would remind them of how their church began. Paul and Silas had been imprisoned because of their ministry. One night, while in chains, they were rejoicing in prison with singing. While they were singing, an earthquake came and opened all the prison cells. The jailor was about to take his life because the prisoners had escaped on his watch. However, none of them left. This caused the jailor to come to faith and led to the establishment of a church. Paul's exhortation to rejoice would remind them that when we rejoice, good things like the beginning of their church, can happen. He then says, know that the Lord is near, even when suffering. We will talk about how close God is to us in Chapter Thirteen.

Now we get to the main point of prayer when we are in difficulty. First, he commands them not to be anxious. I don't know about you, but that can be a hard one for me. I can get anxious about so many things, most of which are not such a big deal. We were lost in Boston one time. I got really uptight. My older daughter said, "Dad, it's not like we're going to die or something!" She was right. If we are all like that with little things, what will we do when we face big things like poverty and persecution? Paul says, "Don't be anxious!" He says, "Rather than get uptight, do everything by prayer." Now I want us to understand that we are to do everything by prayer. We should prayerfully go off to work or school. We should prayerfully go off to church and even off to play. We should pray about everything, but it is particularly true when we are facing some difficulty. In fact, he says, "Do it with thanksgiving." The reason is that when we go to God in prayer about our situation, we are giving it to God. We can be thankful when we give the situation to God because we know that He will take care of it. He will take care of every situation, including our pain, in a way that will bring good and will glorify Himself in a way that will advance His Kingdom.

Paul tells us that when we do that, He will guard our hearts and minds in Christ Jesus. The word "guard" gives the idea of placing a sentinel around us and our situation.[xcvii] So, when we give it to God, we are guarded from anxiety because we become focused upon Jesus. Notice that even if the situation does not change, our attitude changes because our focus is upon Him. He can take care of anything. We know He will change it, or He will give us strength to get through it. In either case, we are at peace knowing that it is in His hands.

A key aspect of this is that when we have placed our situation in God's hands, instead of us seeking to cajole God into doing what we want Him to do, we rest in the fact that He knows best and will do what is best. I remember a decision one of our congregations was going to make. One Wednesday evening, I did my best to convince one of the men who opposed the idea that I preferred, to come around to my way of thinking. I came home and sat quietly and said, "Lord, why do I want this so bad?" As I prayed, I came to the point where I would have been at peace no matter what the decision was. Although the vote passed in the way I preferred (and felt was best for the congregation), I would have been at peace either way.

When our minds get focused upon what God wants, we want what He wants. John tells us that when we know God's will, He answers our prayers. John says,

> *This is the confidence we have in approaching God: that if we ask anything according to his will, he hears us. And if we know that he hears us--whatever we ask--we know that we have what we asked of him* (1 John 5:14-15).

When we give it to God, our hearts get focused upon Jesus, knowing that He knows best. When we reach that point, we become open to God revealing to us what He desires in our situation. When He makes His will known in a situation, if we are committed fully to Him, we will pray that He does what He knows is best.

Sometimes, God may not want to do what we would prefer. You remember the time Paul prayed about his physical problem three times and concluded that God was not going to heal him, but rather demonstrate His power as Paul lived with the situation. As a result, Paul did not pray about healing in that matter again.

At other times, we may know that God wants to remove the situation, either through faith-filled prayers or exercising our spiritual authority.[xcviii] Jesus said,

> *"I tell you the truth, if anyone says to this mountain, 'Go, throw yourself into the sea,' and does not doubt in his heart but believes that what he says will happen, it will be done for him*

(Mark 11:23).

When we become convinced that God wants to remove something because He wants to bless us, or because something is standing in the way of our accomplishing the will of God, then we can pray with confidence and see God do it.

There are times when God does not clearly show us His will. In those cases, we are to give it to Jesus and trust that He will show us what He wants in the situation. We should seek to go through it with the joy of the Lord.

Summary

We have seen how both the Word of God and prayer assist us all the time, but even more so when we are going through difficulty. However, I would encourage you not to wait until things get bad before you begin to become a person of prayer and the Word. If we develop the habits of prayer and getting into the Word of God in our day-to-day lives, we will be more apt to seek Him in the Word and prayer when we have difficulty. In fact, there is a possibility that we will not get into the Word and pray as effectively when we are going through difficulty unless we make these our habits now.

We have already seen a number of the things that God has made available to enable us to fulfill His plan for us. He has forgiven us of our sins (lifting our great burden), and giving us the grace to forgive others (lifting another burden). He has placed the Holy Spirit in our lives -- empowering us to live like Jesus. In this chapter, we have seen that He has given us His Word in order to instruct us in Kingdom living, and has given us the ability to seek Him in prayer in good times, and in times of difficulty.

In Chapter Twelve, we will look at three more provisions that God has made available to enable us to live for Him and to keep plowing when we go through some type of hardship or trauma.

CHAPTER TWELVE
God Spared Nothing – (Part Three)

I have a pastor friend who, when he talks about God providing what we need in order to fulfill the will of God, tells us about his son in the army. He says that his son never has to ask for anything he needs to fulfill his mission. The military takes care of everything to enable him and all his friends to complete their mission, including those times when the troops are facing hardship. The point that my friend makes is that when we seek to do the will of God, He gives us everything we need to fulfill the mission that we have been given.

In the past two chapters, we began to look at some of the key provisions that God has given to us as part of our benefit passage to enable us to keep plowing, even when things get tough. In this chapter, we will talk about three more key provisions that God has given to us. I am sure there are other benefits we could mention, but in these three chapters we will include what I believe are primary keys to our survival under difficult circumstances, and to our fulfilling God's plan for our life.

He Has Given Us The Body Of Christ To Assist
Us In Fulfilling God's Plan

We have been friends with Joe and Suzy[xcix] for over thirty years. We first met them in 1989 when I became their pastor. Joe served on the church Governing Board and the Board of Elders. We were making a number of changes in the church and they always had our backs. Late in our ministry at the church, we went through a very difficult discipline issue. Once again, Joe and Suzy were on board. Joe accompanied me to some very difficult meetings as we sought to resolve the issue biblically.

They continued to be friends and prayer partners even after we resigned from that church. Seven years later, we started KingdomQuest. Immediately, Suzy volunteered to be our administrative assistant. She kept that non-paid position until they moved to another part of the country, and maintained contact with us, prayed for us and the ministry, and have been financial partners. They have been a great support to us, especially at times when things were extremely difficult.

God Calls Christians to Love Each Other in Many Ways.

God has given each of us the Church, the Body of Christ, to participate in our lives and to help us in our pursuit of God. When the Body of Christ is functioning as God desires, it will manifest love (Galatians 5:22-23). Biblical love is a love that desires the benefit of the one being loved. As we walk in the Holy Spirit, we will demonstrate that love to each other. Paul describes love in a well-known passage:

> *Love is patient, love is kind. It does not envy, it does not boast, it is not proud. It is not rude, it is not self-seeking, it is not easily angered, it keeps no record of wrongs. Love does not delight in evil but rejoices with the truth. It always protects, always trusts, always hopes, always perseveres. Love never fails...."* (1Corinthians 13:4-7)

As we read through the New Testament, we find the writers exhorting us to love one another in a variety of ways in what have become known as the "one another" passages. I will list a number of them with their references:

- <u>Be devoted to one another and honor one another</u> (Romans 12:10). It isn't hard to see that Joe and Suzy are devoted to us, and they certainly honored us as their pastor.

- <u>Live in harmony with one another</u> (Romans 12:16).
- <u>Love one another</u> (Romans 13:8 and other passages).
- <u>Don't pass judgment on one another</u> (Romans 14:13).
- <u>Accept one another</u> (Romans 15:7).
- <u>Greet one another with a holy kiss</u> (Romans 16:16 and others). This may seem strange to us as North Americans, but kisses on the cheek are given in many parts of the world. In some parts of the world, men show friendship by holding each other's hands. There are a variety of cultural ways to show respect and love.
- <u>Serve one another</u> (Galatians 5:13).
- <u>Bear with, be patient with one another</u> (Ephesians 4:2).
- <u>Be kind and compassionate with one another</u> (Ephesians 4:32).
- <u>Forgive one another</u> (Ephesians 4:32).
- <u>Worship with one another</u> (Ephesians 5:19).
- <u>Admonish one another</u> (Colossians 3:1).
- <u>Spur each other on</u> (Hebrews 10:24-25). One of the men who served on a board of a church I served in challenged me at times on issues that we discussed. One day, he said, "John, I am hard on you because I see your potential. I want you to reach your full potential."
- <u>Offer hospitality to one another</u> (1 Peter 4:19).
- <u>Although the term "one another" is not there, we are told to give to one another when there is a need</u> (See 2 Corinthians 8-9).

As we become more like Jesus, we will live more and more like this. As we do, we will have friends, who will support us in every way they can. I believe that there should be an increase in these loving activities during times of difficulty.

God Gives Each Believer A Special Role And Special Abilities So That She Can Love Each Other More Effectively.

Suzy, whom I mentioned earlier, had been asked to lead the Women's Missionary Group in our church. She didn't feel that her strongest asset was to lead the group, and that a visionary leader was needed in order to take the group where it needed to go. She came to my wife and said, "Would you lead the group? If you do, I will serve under you. If you tell me where we are headed, I will tell you how to get from point A to point B."

This describes how God designed His Church, the Body of Christ, to function. Paul told the Corinthian believers that God has placed His people into a Body. Read 1 Corinthians 12. He indicates that, just as our physical body has hands, feet, eyes and ears, God has designed the Body of Christ so that each member has a specific role to play. Some of those roles are in the background, some are up front, but each is necessary to enable the Church to fulfill its purpose, to spread the Lord's reign over the entire earth.

He has given a calling and supernatural abilities for every believer.

We have already discussed that fact that God has created each of us to fulfill a specific purpose (Ephesians 2:10). This ought to encourage every one of us. No one is an accident. God designed us to fulfill a purpose and, as I like to tell our *Breaking Free* students, it is bigger than you think! Paul told the church in Ephesus,

> *Now to him who is able to do immeasurably more than all we ask or imagine, according to his power that is at work within us...* (Ephesians 3:20).

As we consider our wildest dreams (dreams that are placed in us by God), we see that God wants to do immeasurably more than what we can imagine at this particular time. Not only has He called us, but He has also given us spiritual gifts (supernatural, Holy Spirit-given abilities) to coincide with our calling, so that we can are empowered to play the role God has for us. (See the lists in 1 Corinthians 12:7-10 and Romans 12:6-8).[c] We have a dear friend named Pam. She came to Christ after a tragedy happened at her home. She has exercised a gift of giving to us personally for years, giving both funds and products. She recently became ill and has been unable to work for some time. She has a very close friend, Jane, who has some administrative gifts and has helped Pam do her taxes and apply for various government programs during her time of illness. She has spent many hours on these projects. This is an example of how someone uses their gifts to assist people in a time of hardship.

We also know a lady, Joanne, from one of the churches where we minister on a frequent basis. Joanne comes from another country, therefore she has an amazing ministry of both teaching and mercy to people who have moved to the U.S. from other countries. She teaches them English and she and her husband do many things to help them. She is helping people at a time of hardship and she is sharing Christ with them. These examples only give a small portion of the abilities that God gives to His children throughout the earth. Each gift is given to complement people's various callings and personalities. God does this to give each believer a significant role in Kingdom-advance.

Many people are needed for each ministry. *KingdomQuest* is a very small ministry, yet we depend upon our board, our donors, and those committed to praying for us. In addition, we have people who assist us in a variety of ways: We have been blessed with a number of people who have given us computers, fixed our computers and helped us with web design. There are people who care for us and support us in many ways. Everyone of them plays a key role in what we do. Every one of them has played a major role in everything God has done through KingdomQuest.

God gives leaders to train and organize His Body.

> *It was he who gave some to be apostles, some to be prophets, some to be evangelists, and some to be pastors and teachers, to prepare God's people for works of service, so that the body of Christ may be built up... (Ephesians 4:11-12).*

These verses tell us that God has raised up five offices (leadership gifts) in order to equip people to serve the Lord. These leaders function in their differing areas to train believers in their callings and their gifts, and then place them where they will fit best. In some cases this means releasing them to other ministries. God called me to serve as a pastor in a small university town in Pennsylvania. While I was there, a new pastor came to our church. We became great friends. He began to place me in positions of leadership. He let me loose to teach Sunday School and at times, allowed me to preach during the Sunday evening services.

When I finally put out the idea that I felt God was calling me to be a pastor, he supported me from day one, which meant that I would be leaving his church where I had been a support to him.

You may wonder what this has to do with suffering. First of all, many members of the Body of Christ will care for us when we are hurting, with the love placed in them by the Holy Spirit. In addition, God has gifted some members of the Body with gifts of mercy, giving and counseling. There are also those who can pray in faith for the sick. When these leaders who have given themselves to training people and helping them develop their gifts become aware of those in the congregation with needs, they will put those with needs together with those with gifts, to bring help to them. These leaders will also set up other ministries, like benevolent funds, to minister to hurting people.

God has provided a loving family to encourage us in good times and to care for us when we are in need.

God Has Deputized Us

Then Jesus came to them and said, "All authority in heaven and on earth has been given to me. Therefore go and make disciples of all nations, baptizing them in the name of the Father and of the Son and of the Holy Spirit, and teaching them to obey everything I have commanded you. And surely I am with you always, to the very end of the age (Matthew 28:18-20).

As Jesus was getting ready to leave His disciples and go back to heaven to be with His Father, He told them that all authority had been given to Him. The word authority has to do with "delegated influence, authority, and jurisdiction."[ci] He was given this authority because of what He did when He died and rose from the dead. Because He has been given all authority, He now deputizes whomever He wants to do whatever He wants. He deputized the twelve, and all disciples after them to go and disciple every ethnic group in the world. When they go, they go with His authority as subjects go forth when given authority by their king.

Let me illustrate how this works. Imagine someone being deputized as a police offer. He (or she) is given the authority which is represented by his badge. Now imagine that officer puts on his uniform. When the officer puts his hand up to stop a car, the car stops. He doesn't have the power to stop the car, but when he exercises his authority the car stops. If the car decides not to stop, the officer has the power of the government standing behind him, and the power standing behind the police officer will come to bear against the offender. They will be caught and prosecuted.

Now imagine the same police officer standing in the road in his or her personal clothing and hold up his hand to stop a car. The car may not stop because as a civilian, he has no right to stop the car and he doesn't have the physical power to stop it.

As believers, we don't have the power to change our community and our world. However, God does. God has given us His power in two ways. First, He has empowered us by the Holy Spirit in the ways we have discussed earlier in the book. Secondly, He has endowed us with His authority which enables us to put a stop to activity that is hindering His work.

Before we begin to talk about our authority in Christ, we need to understand the power that is behind that authority. Paul told the Ephesian church that he had three truths he wanted them to understand. He said he wanted them to know

> *his incomparably great power for us who believe. That power is like the working of his mighty strength, which he exerted in Christ when he raised him from the dead and seated him at his right hand in the heavenly realms, far above all rule and authority, power and dominion, and every title that can be given, not only in the present age but also in the one to come. And God placed all things under his feet and appointed him to be head over everything for the church, which is his body, the fullness of him who fills everything in every way (Ephesians 1:19-23).*

First, Paul prays that they would know the hope that is in Jesus. We have talked about this when we discussed that God wants to do more in us and through us as we live here on earth, and so much more when enter eternity with Him. Secondly, Paul wants them to understand the great inheritance that Jesus has in the saints. This inheritance includes the billions who have, and will, come to Him as we fulfill His vision to reach every people group. It also includes every personal victory and every effective ministry accomplished by every one of those believers. Thirdly, Paul wants them to understand the power that is behind them, as they go out as authorized deputies of Jesus, seeking to advance His Kingdom.

In order for us to minister for Him in danger and through suffering, we must understand how much power He possesses. Paul tells us the extent of that power in the passage. It helps us because we seem to like to know how much power things have. We tell how much horsepower is under the hood of our car. During the cold war between the U.S. and the U.S.S.R. in the 1950's and 1960's, each nation was testing nuclear weapons. When the blast went off, each nation would tell how many mega tons of power had been set off.

Paul tells us that the power that is available to us is like the power that God exercised when He raised Jesus from the dead. I believe we can safely assume that Satan had all his firepower at the tomb between Friday and Sunday because if he could have stopped Jesus' resurrection, he would have defeated God, won the battle for the hearts of men, and would have permanently become the prince of this world. In spite of Satan's best efforts, God had sufficient power to raise Jesus from the dead and still be infinitely powerful.

He has all power -- enough power so that every believer in every age has enough power behind them to accomplish everything God has deputized us to do:

He has given us the authority to bind (forbid) and loose (allow).

On one occasion, Jesus took His disciples to Caesarea Philippi for a very important time. He asked them who men said He was. They told Him what others were saying. Then He asked them the all-important question. He asked them who THEY said He was. Peter declared:

> *"You are the Christ, the Son of the Living God!" Jesus replied, "And I tell you that you are Peter, and on this rock I will build my church, and the gates of Hades will not overcome it. I will give you the keys of the kingdom of heaven; whatever you bind on earth will be bound in heaven, and whatever you loose on earth will be loosed in heaven" (Matthew 16:18-19).*

Jesus had specifically chosen this location. It was a place of pagan worship and a place with a deep well that some called the Gate of Hades. Jesus declared that He would build His church everywhere including this place, the very Gates of Hades.

He then told Peter that He had given him the keys of the kingdom, indicating that with those keys he had the power to loose (allow) and bind (forbid). This passage seems to indicate that whatever we bind or loose on earth will be bound or loosed in heaven. However, an alternative translation of this passage gives us the proper understanding. The Amplified Bible says,

> *"I will give you the keys of the kingdom of heaven; and whatever you bind (declare to be improper and unlawful) on earth must be what is already bound in heaven; and whatever you loose (declare lawful) on earth must be what is already loosed in heaven"*[cii]

I believe that this is the correct translation, because without God's input, we would never know what to forbid or allow. Our task is to walk so closely with God that He reveals what He wants forbidden and what He wants allowed.

Paul King tells a story that occurred in China in 1924. Robert Jaffrey, a well-known missionary, and another missionary set out to rescue some missionaries that had been taken captive. They were also both taken captive. A week later, Jaffrey and another missionary were released. A few weeks later, another missionary, Rex Ray escaped leaving one missionary, Edgar Carne, captive. King says that on June 20, those praying received faith in prayer, to declare the missionary loosed. He was released that very day.[ciii] As the intercessors loosed Mr. Carne in prayer, he was physically released to minister again, and was released from his suffering by the authority of Christ.

Binding and loosing are helpful to us as we seek to do the will of God. As we discern from the Holy Spirit that something is hindering the work of God, we can bind or loose it depending upon the need. This would include binding every demonic spirit that blinds the eyes of unbelievers. If we are praying for the lost, we can bind the evil spirits which blind them (2 Corinthians 4:4). This does not automatically mean that people will be saved, but it does free them to make a decision for Christ without demonic interference. Binding and loosing also applies to our suffering when we discern from the Lord that our sickness, rejection, or persecution is hindering the work of God. We must be sure that God has led us to loose ourselves from a situation, or bind those causing us pain, because God may be using the situation, at least for a time, to develop our character.

He gives us authority to help people get deliverance from demonic bondage.

I would encourage you to get our manual, ***Breaking Free to Your Destiny***, [civ] for a fuller discussion of this subject. We have seen people gain some amazing freedom as we have cast demons out of them. Let me give you a brief account of how we handle this. First, we believe that, generally, deliverance happens effectively when the person is a believer in Jesus Christ. If the person we are attempting to help is not a believer, we seek do our best to lead them to Christ. The reason is that Jesus sets people free to serve Him, so we want to make sure that when a person gains freedom, he or she is committed to serving Him and His purposes. Secondly, we help the person seeking freedom to repent of their known sins. As God reveals areas where the person seeking deliverance needs to repent, we lead them through the process. Persistent sin is often what gives the spirit the right to hold a person in bondage. When the person repents, the spirit loses its right to hold on to the person. When the demons' rights have been exposed and repented of, we as believers can order the demonic spirits to leave. (See the "Personal Evaluation" to assist with repentance and the "Prayer of Renunciation", both in *Breaking Free*.)

We ministered *Breaking Free* in a small city in India. One of the participants was a shy girl named Martha. She was so paralyzed by fear, she couldn't talk or pray publicly. She confessed her fear. We commanded it to go, and when we had time for testimonies, Martha stood up with a beaming smile and shared for a long time. The people hearing her testimony could not believe it was Martha, because she had been so shy!

On another occasion, two men approached me separately, both within a week. One had fathered a child as a teenager. He repented, but when he was with his wife, he felt like the mother of his child from his teen years was with them. He had asked for forgiveness, but was tortured with the past relationship. A second man approached me. He had been unfaithful to his wife with many women, but he had come to Christ and only wanted to be with his wife. He also repented, but continually saw the faces of women he had been with. He wanted freedom. In both cases, we took our place of authority in Christ, and broke emotional, demonic ties (soul ties) with other women. They both came back the next week completely delivered from their tormenting thoughts.

As God shows us that some of our suffering (caused by emotional or physical sickness, lack of work, etc.) is an attack from the enemy, we can take our place of authority and stop his work by binding and loosing, as God directs. As we do this, we will see situations change. Please remember that we bind and loose only in those areas that God clearly shows us are from the enemy. Some difficulties may be like Paul's sickness, designed to demonstrate God's grace as Paul walked in victory in spite of his illness. (2 Corinthians 12:9)

God Provides For All Of Our Needs

We have seen in Chapters 10-12 that God meets all our needs. He has provided His Word, prayer, the Church of Jesus Christ, authority in Christ, the Holy Spirit, and forgiveness of sins and the grace to forgive others. He also meets our financial needs.

I have talked about God's faithfulness in meeting our financial needs throughout the book. However, I wanted to bring some principles and examples together here, in one place.

God meets our needs

"And my God will meet all your needs according to his glorious riches in Christ Jesus" (Philippians 4:19).

Paul is explaining that God meets our needs out of His riches in Christ Jesus. He has unlimited resources. He has enough to meet our personal needs and ministry needs. David tells us, *"I was young and now I am old, yet I have never seen the righteous forsaken or their children begging bread"* (Psalms 37:25).

I could tell you many stories of how God provided for our family of four while I attended seminary, even miraculously providing Christmas gifts and vacations. He also provided for us for three months, while we were between pastoral positions. I could also tell you stories of how He has met the needs of our non-profit ministry, KingdomQuest, even as He has led us to rarely ask people for funds, only Him. However, I want to tell you some stories from people that I know.

We have a pastor friend in India, Sanjay. He went from being a pastor to being a district leader. He needed a vehicle. He wanted a vehicle large enough to take leaders and young pastors with him for mentoring and decision making. While he was in the U.S., a doctor asked him what he needed. He decided to be bold and say, "a vehicle." The doctor asked how much it cost in India. Sanjay told him. In a few months the money arrived. The next time we went to India, we were picked up in the new vehicle. We had the privilege of being the first guests to ride in it.

During a trip to Indonesia, our team fell in love with the worship leader. Her warn out shoes looked too big. The ladies got together and gave her money, thinking she would buy shoes.

She was amazed at the provision. She said, "Praise God! I can eat next week." She had saved enough money to travel to a conference, but had no money for food. She was going to fast during the conference, but God met her need for food (and shoes) through the ladies on our team.

A third story is amazing. A pastor friend, Manish, had been meeting with his people under a tree; not a pleasant task in the rainy season. He met a man from a different religion who had a wedding hall which people rented for weddings and other events. The man recognized Manish even though they had never met. He explained that he had had a dream where he saw Manish speaking to people who were under a tree while it was raining. The man said, "you can use my wedding hall for services when I don't have a wedding," which did not often happen on Sunday. We spoke to groups of leaders on several occasions at the wedding hall because of the generosity of this man. The man even used his contacts to get top of the line meals at a discounted price.

Some Key Principles Of Giving Which Will Assist Us In Seeing Our Needs Met:

"Give, and it will be given to you. A good measure, pressed down, shaken together and running over, will be poured into your lap. For with the measure you use, it will be measured to you" (Luke 6:38).

In this passage, Jesus tells us that God gives to us with the measure that we give. I often use this illustration in India. When we take a bath many places in India, they bring us a large bucket of warm water and then bring a very small bucket used to get water from the large bucket and pour it over ourselves. Pointing to the two buckets, I ask them, "Do you want to be blessed from the small bucket or the big bucket?" With the measure we give, God will bless us. They want to be blessed from the big one, and so do we!

We must understand that God's blessing does not come

from the raw amount we give. Some have much more to give, and a large sum may not be a sacrifice. Others sacrifice greatly by giving a little. Remember the woman who put in two coins? Jesus said that she gave the most because she, out of her limited resources, gave it all (Mark 12:42). So, the first principle is to be generous as God leads us.

However, there is another principle that I believe is key in seeing God meet our needs. It is the principle of tithing. This means we give a tenth. I personally believe that it is a tenth off the amount of income prior to taxes. Malachi told the Jewish people. *"Will a man rob God? Yet you rob me. But you ask, 'How do we rob you?' In tithes and offerings"* (Malachi 3:8). This verse implies that the first 10% belongs to God. You may ask, "Does God need it?" He does not, but we need to give so that we demonstrate that we trust Him. It makes no sense to our natural mind, but when we give our tithe, God will miraculously meet our needs. So, I encourage you to give a tithe of your money to the work of the Lord and be generous as He leads us beyond that. He promises to meet our needs!

God did not spare Jesus. Therefore, He will not spare anything else we need whether we are going through normal times or if we are experiencing hardship. Are you going through hardship? Forgive, if you have those you need to forgive. Allow the Holy Spirit to control your life. Seek His Word for answers to your situation, and pray. Look for those who can help you in the Body of Christ. Exercise authority as God directs, and expect God to meet you in whatever you need. In this way, we can plow forward in good times and when we are experiencing hardship and suffering. God has not spared anything, and we cannot outgive Him!

CHAPTER THIRTEEN
Nothing Can Separate Us From God

If you live in a Western country, there is nothing I can do to describe the local trains in Mumbai, India, unless you have been there. I believe that each car has seating for 36-40 people. Usually, 45-60 people sit in them. In addition, every aisle is filled with people, including the aisles between the seats on each side. They did not announce the next exit, at least when we were there, so as Americans we had no idea where we should get off the train. My plan was to stay as close to my traveling companion as possible so that I would get on and off the train when he did. I did not want anything to separate me from my guide. I am grateful that I never got separated from my friend.

Once a pastor's wife got Kerry on the "women's car" (In India, they have women only cars on the trains for modesty), but she did not make it on the car. Kerry was separated from our guide. (Fortunately, Kerry was with another woman heading to the meeting where Kerry would speak.)

No matter how hard I tried to stay with my Indian friend, it would have been possible to get separated. However, the fifth provision God has for those who are suffering is that nothing can separate us from the love of Christ (See Romans 8:35-39). It is always good to know this, but it is especially important to us when we are going through difficulty. We may be going through a particularly tough round of chemotherapy and wonder where God is. We may be a believer suffering in prison for his or her faith, who may wonder where God is. We may be experiencing rejection from someone close like a spouse, a child or sister. In our state of rejection, we wonder if God has rejected us as well. Paul assures us that He is there no matter who is hurting us or what we are going through. Nothing can separate us from God!

But What About This?

It seems impossible that nothing can separate us from God's love. Sometimes, we hear a truth like this one and think, "This can't be possible. What about...?" Paul seems to anticipate that people would come up with "what if's." As a result, he spends several verses discussing difficulties that we may believe have the potential to separate us from God's love. In the next few pages we will look at some of these.

Trouble

Albert Barnes tells us that the word "trouble" generally means pressure from without.[cv] We face many types of pressure from the outside. We may be bullied by someone at work or school, or we may face intense peer pressure. We may have a boss with unrealistic expectations, or feel that we must keep up with cultural economic standards or morals. Of course, we could come up with many scenarios depicting pressure from the outside. We may think that God has abandoned us as we go through these difficulties. Paul says, "Trouble can't separate us from God!"

Hardship

Barnes explains that "hardship" occurs when everything seems to be closing in on us and we do not know what to do.[cvi] Hardship can appear in many of life's situations. It will depend upon our ability to trust God and handle stress. However, a serious illness or injury could qualify as a hardship. How will I take care of my family? Will I be able to find another job since I can't continue to do my job? Or we may realize that our family is falling apart. What can I do to cope or what can I do to mend the situation? Any situation that causes us to throw our hands in the air and wonder "what do I do now?" is a hardship. Paul tells us once again, hardship will not separate us from God!

Persecution

We experience persecution when we are attacked for our faith. For some it may be rejection or ridicule. In some places in the world, persecution may involve being disowned by your family, or being beaten, tortured, raped, imprisoned, or killed. We met a pastor, who lived through a communist dictatorship. He spent time in prison. He had a groove in his shoulder blade from torture. He would tell you that persecution does not separate us from God's love. He is still serving as a pastor, with an evangelist's heart and a heart for orphans.

Famine

Famine ravages a land and the people who live in that land. Jacob and his family experienced famine that would have killed his family, and ultimately the future people of Israel, if God had not provided for them through Joseph, who was prime minister of Egypt. People in famine may wonder if God is there. They cannot grow food, their animals are dying, and the economy of their region is dying. Paul says, "Famine can't separate us from God's love."

Danger

This refers to any type of danger. God may ask us to go into dangerous situations, in our own country or some other place in the world, in order to minister. People who live in those places need Jesus as well. We have heard many stories of evangelists in India going into villages that have never heard of Jesus, and being severely beaten for desiring to preach the Gospel. Believers around the world go into dangerous situations in order to preach the Gospel. Of course, we can face danger as we go into a delicate surgery, or even as we seek to reconcile with someone who has been belligerent toward us. These kinds of situations are dangerous because we do not know how the other person will react to our attempts to reconcile. No danger can separate us from God's love!

Sword

This could mean war time and it can mean those who have judicial power. The latter would be when we have been arrested and facing the justice system for doing the will of God.[cvii] Even war and belligerent judicial systems cannot separate us from the Love of God.

Paul's list covers about every possible situation we could find ourselves in. Paul says, in no uncertain terms, these cannot separate us from the love of God. But someone says, "That is great, but what about...? Yes, Paul, you've told me about situations that can happen in my life, but I still have a few more questions before I can believe nothing can separate me from Christ's love. For instance..."

Life and death

We have come to Christ during our life on earth. Therefore, when we die, will we be separated from God? The answer is no. We talked about the eternal home of believers in chapter six. We will be far more alive then than we are now. The New Heaven and New Earth will be amazing. We will go from being corruptible to incorruptible. We will no longer be capable of sinning. We will be new. We will also be eternally in the presence of God, closer than we can get while we are on earth. Death will not separate us from God, but bring us closer. All of the verses above and below indicate that nothing can separate us from God's love in this life.

Angels and demons

But there is a place where someone has testified: ***"What*** *is man that you are mindful of him, the son of man that you care for him? You made him a little lower than the angels; you crowned him with glory and honor"* (Hebrews 2:6-7). The bottom line is that God has made man a little lower than angels. This would include the world of demons as well.[cviii] If these beings are greater than mankind, and the demons hate humans, can't they do something to separate us from God? Paul says, "No!" "Can you understand it? Nothing can separate us from the Love of God in Christ."

Present and future

We are not going to do anything now or in our future to cause God to withdraw from us. He has forgiven us of our sin, and He has made provision for us to repent when we sin. There are not going to be natural disasters, wars, plagues, pandemics that have the power to separate us from God now or in the future.

Powers and anything in creation

("principalities" is how KJV interprets "demons" in the NIV)

The powers and principalities could refer to those in civil authority. They may tell us that we cannot worship, and even bull doze our churches (as has been happening in some parts of the world), but they cannot separate us from God. I told you the story of our pastor friend whose building was burned down. He did not have his building, but he came to our meeting and was met by God. He was changed by the power of God. Even without his building, he went back to his city and had an outdoor service where the church had been. They were even protected by the police. He came to our second meeting the next week filled with the joy of the Lord. He was not separated from God's love. Neither can we.

Neither height nor depth

These would seem to indicate the state of life that a person finds themselves in. They may gain notoriety or wealth. This does not separate them from God's love. A person may be considered low by the standards of the world. This can't separate one from God's love. We have known believers of high standard and those with little who had great walk with the Lord.

In the middle of listing these various means that some might think could separate us from God's love, Paul says, "*No, in all these things we are more than conquerors through him who loved us*" (Romans 8:37). The Greek word for the phrase "more than conquerors" is "*hupernikao*." "*Nikao*" is the word for conqueror. This word indicates that we have gone beyond "normal" conquering. Paul says, "even if we experience hardships, or are resisted by demons or civil leaders, we can keep plowing. We can finish the race that God set out for us, even in the midst of difficulty." Paul says, "We can do this! We can win this war! We are hyper conquerors."

Some who are wondering if this good news is really true might say, "Well, I know that I can have victory in all these areas, but what about Jesus? Could I do something that would cause Jesus to condemn me? Paul tells us that this is not even logical. He says, "Why would Jesus condemn us? He died to bring us to God. He rose to provide a new life. Besides that, He prays for us to recognize that He is always with them! He sits at the right hand of God and prays that we will understand all that He has provided for us to endure hardship and fulfill His plan for our life. We can keep plowing as we seek to do His will because He is with us and has provided all we need" (Romans 8:34). It is not likely that Jesus is going to give up on us. He will not! NOTHING CAN SEPARATE US FROM THE LOVE OF GOD EXPRESSED IN CHRIST JESUS.

So Let's Walk Close To Him

There is nothing that can separate us from His love. This

does not suggest that we cannot do things that hinder the quality of our walk with God. He still loves us even if our walk with Him cools down. However, He still prays for us and wants us to be more than conquerors.

It has been a long time since I attended a wedding that had the "traditional" wedding vows. It may be the same for us. In case you forgot, here is how they go:

"I, _______, take thee, _______, to be my wedded wife/husband, to have and to hold from this day forward, for better, for worse, for richer, for poorer, in sickness and in health, to love and to cherish, till death do us part, according to God's holy ordinance; and thereto I pledge thee my faith."[cix]

When you think of it, these are pretty hefty commitments. They communicate that no matter what happens I want to be with you. Good things can happen, but what is really important is that I am living life with you. On the other hand, bad things might happen, but what is really important is that I am with you. When a couple makes these vows or ones that are similar, they are saying to each other that you are more important than anything else. I will go through what life brings if I can be with you.

Paul tells us that he sees his relationship with God that way. He says,

But whatever was to my profit I now consider loss for the sake of Christ. What is more, I consider everything a loss compared to the surpassing greatness of knowing Christ Jesus my Lord, for whose sake I have lost all things. I consider them rubbish, that I may gain Christ" (Philippians 3:7-8)"

Paul had attained great status in Judaism. He was a rising star, having been mentored by an important rabbi. However, when he come to Christ, he became persona-non-grata among Jews. He had many difficulties, ranging from shipwreck to persecution and imprisonment, as he planted churches all over the empire, He says, "This is okay. I have Christ! I have given up all my notoriety for Him. It was well worth it."

In fact, in his letter to the Ephesians, Paul likens the marriage relationship with the relationship of Christ to His Church. When we enter into a relationship with Jesus, we are committing ourselves to be faithful to Him throughout our life. We are saying that we will keep plowing in every situation because the most important thing to us is that we get to go through life with the Lord.

As we have already seen, God has kept His part of the bargain. We saw that nothing can separate us from God. In fact, he makes the promise to us, *"God has said, 'Never will I leave you; never will I forsake you'"* (Hebrews 13:5). Literally, God is saying that I will never desert you and never leave you behind.[cx]

The question for us, then, is what can we do to help insure that we keep our part of our vow to live life with and for God until we go to be with Him. In the remainder of the chapter, we will outline some ways that we can remain faithful to the Lord and get to know Him in the process.

Living In An Attitude Of Worship

He is infinitely valuable

If we look back at the Philippians 3 passage, we find that when Paul considered all his accomplishments and all that he accomplished in his life, nothing came close to knowing Christ. There is no one greater than Father, Son and Holy Spirit. God is holy, meaning that He is incomparably greater than creation. He has always existed! He is infinite in every quality, which includes love, mercy, grace, power, and wisdom. He lacks nothing! No one could ever love us so much or care for us so deeply. He is worthy to be worshipped. Therefore, our attitude toward Him should be there is no greater privilege than knowing Him and there is no price to great to get to know Him and serve Him.

He is awesome! He is wonderful! He is God and He is my heavenly Father! We need to walk in this kind of intimacy and awe at all times. However, where we are going through hardships, suffering and persecution, we desperately need to walk close to Him. We need to stay close to him, like I stayed with my Indian guide on the train in times of difficulty. We will not know how to walk through these times unless we must gaze upon His greatness and cling to Him as He takes us through difficulty.

We need Him to walk in true righteousness - Paul told the Philippians that he wanted the righteousness that comes from Christ, not one that comes from the law. He tells them that no has a better reason to boast about earned righteousness than him. Paul had kept every aspect of the law, as much as possible. He had tasted of human righteousness. It had left him empty. He said, "I count my own righteousness as rubbish. It is not all that it claims to be. Remember his remarks from Romans 7. He said, "I don't do what I want, but do what I do not want to do." He said, "I need to be delivered from this!" (See Romans 7:14-25). He then tells us what the Holy Spirit did for him and what He can do for us. He says, "The righteousness that I had on my own wasn't really righteousness. It was not until the Holy Spirit entered into me that I began to understand true, God-sent righteousness.

We especially need His righteousness living in us during times of suffering. We can become frustrated and disillusioned that things are not going the way we desire. We can become angry or depressed. If we are walking close to Him with His righteousness flowing in and through our lives, we can walk through these difficult times in a more righteous manner. Perhaps this is why Peter could be sound asleep in prison, even when he was scheduled for execution (Acts 12), or how Paul and Silas could be having a worship service while chained in prison (Acts 16). I don't know about you, but I want to be able to react in a proper way. I know that I can't even walk righteously through little things without Him.

We need to know Him to walk in faith

The writer of Hebrews tells us,

> *Now faith is being sure of what we hope for and certain of what we do not see"* (Hebrews 11:1)

> *And without faith it is impossible to please God, because anyone who comes to him must believe that he exists and that he rewards those who earnestly seek him* (Hebrews 11:6).

He is making it quite clear that we will only please God when we live by faith. It takes faith in order to be more like Jesus. We must believe that He can work in such a way that we go from being like we are in our own flesh to becoming like Jesus. We will only minister effectively when we believe that God can have an impact upon others through us. We will never exercise faith until we get a glimpse of Him that elevates our faith to believe Him.

At the end of John's Gospel, he tells his readers why he wrote his Gospel. He says,

> *Jesus did many other miraculous signs in the presence of his disciples, which are not recorded in this book. But these are written that you may believe that Jesus is the Christ, the Son of God, and that by believing you may have life in his name"* (John 20:30-31).

John tells his readers that he could have written about many things that he saw happen in Jesus life. John says, "there are many miracles that He performed that I did not choose to write about. However, I chose the ones that I did for two reasons. First, I wrote so that you would believe that Jesus is the Christ. I wanted you to know that He is the One that came from God. I wanted you to enter into a relationship with Him! I wanted you to be born again, saved!"

"Secondly, I wanted you to have life in His name." Whenever the Scriptures talk of the name of God, or the name of Jesus, it means that God has revealed Himself is such a way that the fresh glimpse we received has been so etched in our inner selves that we will never be the same. When Abraham saw the ram in the bushes that God provided for the sacrifice, he exclaimed that God is the God who provides (Genesis 22:14). Abraham recognized like never before that God provides. I doubt that he had a problem believing God for provision in the future.

Moses and the Jewish people came upon some water that was not suitable to drink. The Lord told Moses to throw a branch of a tree into the water. The water became potable. Using this as an example, God said, "I am the God who heals" (Exodus 15:26). There are situations like this where God gives us a "revelation"[cxi] of who He is. When we get this kind of revelation of God, our faith comes alive. When our faith comes alive, we trust God in ways we never did before. We come alive in a new way. As we get to know God, we come alive because we will trust this awesome God for more of what He has provided for us.

We need these revelations of God in order to grow in our walk with God.

However, we need even greater clarity when we are suffering. In fact, we may get a greater revelation of God when going through hardship. It is during those times that we need a ram in the bush or fresh water. We recently went to an appointment. There was a young woman there with her baby. She told us that her husband had recently been healed of a stage 4 renal disease. He went from a serious illness to not being sick at all. Hallelujah! God is the Healer. They will never forget that.

As we remain in an attitude of worship, recognizing Him for His greatness, we will be blessed and energized by His presence and He will impart righteousness and life to us. How do we maintain that kind of relationship with God as we make our way through life's ups and downs?

Developing And Maintaining An Alive Relationship With God

You must be born again.

When Nicodemus, a religious leader in Jesus' time, came to Jesus, He told him that in order to see the Kingdom of God he had to be born again. We have talked about this in various ways in the book, but Jesus meant that in order to see the truths that will enable us to live like God desires, we must receive Christ into our lives as our personal Lord and Savior. If you have never received Christ, I recommend that you reread chapter five and pray the prayer at the end of the chapter.

Give your life fully to Jesus.

God will reveal Himself to those who have determined that they want to live their life fully for Him. If you have never committed your life fully to Him, again, I recommend that you reread chapter five and pray the prayer at the end.

Spend time with God.

We often hear stories of couples who got married expecting a life of bliss as they started life on their wedding day. Twenty-five years later, the children are raised and when they look at each other across the table, they see a stranger. If we are going to have an alive relationship with God, we must spend time with Him. We can even get so busy with ministry that we fail to continue to have a relationship with the One for whom we are ministering.

So, I recommend:

Set time aside each day to read the Bible and pray.

If we are too busy to spend time with God, we are too busy. As we approach our time with God, let's look at it as a conversation. Begin with some worship. It does not need to be singing, although you may want to sing. You can use words to focus upon His greatness. This will help you to recognize whose presence you are entering. Then have a time in the Word of God, the Bible. As you begin to read the Word of God, ask God to speak to you in any way that He desires. He may speak to you about a situation in your life, or He may want to help you make a decision, or avoid some sin. He may also want to encourage you. Lastly, pray about what He has said as well as other requests that He lays upon your heart.

Engage in fellowship with other believers.

As you spend time with other believers in casual fellowship, such as in Bible Studies or in a church meeting, share what God is doing in your life and openly share some of the struggles you may have. As we do this, we will get to know God as we hear how others are getting to know Him. Of course, we get to know Him as we hear the Word of God taught and preached. When someone else is sharing the Word, ask God to speak to you in the same way you do during your personal time with God.

Obey what God is saying to you. As we obey God, He will find us faithful and reveal more of Himself. Sometimes we only get to know God when we obey. We had a young couple in one of the churches that we served in. One of our visitation teams led them to Christ. A few weeks later, they decided that they we going to begin to tithe, even though they did not know how that would work out for them financially. A few weeks later, they shared that they had begun to tithe and had more money left at the end of the month than before. They said, they did not know how that happened, but it did. A few months later, he was at seminary and became a military chaplain. They heard! They obeyed! They got a revelation of the living God and God revealed more, which they obeyed, leading to more revelation of Him and more fruitful ministry.

In Summary

We may wonder where God is when we are going through difficulty. There is no situation or no person that can separate us from God's love. He is faithful!

We can get to know that God in an intimate way. As we do, He reveals Himself to us in ways that shake us in a good way and energize our faith. Let's commit ourselves to a life of getting to know Him. If you are going through difficulty spend time with Him. If you are in a period that is not so hard, get to know Him so that if things get tough you will know Him and know that you can trust Him then. He can change the situation, or He can get you through it. He is awesome! He wants you to get to know Him and He wants to walk through the difficulty with you. Set an appointment with Him today.

EPILOGUE

God sent His Son to pay the price for our sin and give us a new life that includes fulfilling His original plan for humans to spread God's reign throughout the earth. (See Genesis 1:28 and Matthew 28:18-20). God desires that everyone who has received Christ as Lord and Savior gives their life to playing their part in taking His Kingdom to the world. In fact, Jesus said,

> *"No one who puts his hand to the plow and looks back is fit for service in the kingdom of God"* (Luke 9:62).

However, this task is not always easy. As believers, we face obstacles that distract us from fulfilling the will of God for our lives. In fact, immediately after Paul told the believers in Rome about the wonderful way the Holy Spirit empowers us to live for God, he tells them and us that we will only access the benefits of being a co-heir with Christ if we suffer with Him. Perhaps that shocks you as much as it did for me six years ago. However, as we saw in the early chapters of this book, suffering can come in a variety of ways from a number of sources. In fact, the New Testament writers mention suffering more than 100 times in 18 New Testament books.

Perhaps you are experiencing some type of suffering at this time. It may be an illness, or a loss of a job or relationship. It may have come from a natural disaster, or some form of persecution. As you go through these difficulties, you may be asking how you can bear up under the hardship and continue to keep plowing for the Lord.

Fortunately, Paul not only told the Roman believers that they would experience sufferings, but he gave them five keys to assisting them to make it through their hardship. Let me review:

Think about eternity

Paul tells us that thinking of our future in eternity, can assist us to hang on and keep plowing. In Chapter Six, we talked about the wonders of the New Heaven and New Earth, the fact that we will change and become incorruptible, incapable of sinning in any way and most importantly, we will dwell in the presence of God, Himself.

As we go through difficultly, God prays for us.

In Chapter Seven, we talked about the fact that both the Holy Spirit and Jesus pray for us not only to get through difficulty, but that we will fulfill God's complete plan for our life.

God brings good out of bad situations.

In Chapters Eight and Nine, we explored a number of ways that God brings good out of our hardships. Not the least of which is that He increases our ability to minister to others (I Corinthians 1:3-4). Of course, God sometimes miraculously rescues us from these situations, in ways such as changing the weather, healing us, or changing situations (See Matthew 8).

God provides all we need to fulfill His will in our lives.

We spent three chapters (10-12) discussing the marvelous provisions that God has given us so that we can fulfill His will even when we go through difficulty.

In Chapter Thirteen, we saw that God remains faithful to us under every possible circumstance.

So, What Do I Do?

As we consider the above truths, I recommend the following as we come to the close of *Finishing Strong*. First, do everything you can to develop an intimate relationship with God. (See Chapter Thirteen for more details). Seek Him in His Word daily. It is in the Word that we learn truth, and where we find the promises of God that assist us to put on the divine nature (2 Peter 1:3-4). If you are not going through difficulty, this is a perfect time to get to know Him. However, if you are, He may want to use this time to assist you to get to know Him better.

Secondly, become a person of prayer. You can talk to God about anything. If you would like to have a model to begin your prayer life, look at the Lord's Prayer in Matthew 6:9-13 or Luke 11:2-4.

Thirdly, learn to walk in the Holy Spirit's power and direction. He gives us God's wisdom. He will help us to understand our situation. He may even reveal to us what He is doing in the situation we are facing. If not, He will empower you to make it through. If you are not sure how to do this, seek out a believer who knows how to listen to and obey the Holy Spirit. They will help you.

Fourthly, keep your eyes on God's target for your life on earth, and His target for you for eternity.[cxii] As part of this, ask God to show you ways to be used of Him in your difficulty, and ask Him what He is seeking to teach you in your difficulty. This will allow God to prepare you for the future He has for you here and there.

Cling to God always! Especially cling to Him when you are suffering! As you do, He will use you in amazing ways and someday He will greet you with a "Well done, good and faithful servant!"

ACKNOWLEDGE-MENTS

It is impossible to name everyone who had an impact in the producing of *Finishing Strong.* There have been many men who have served as my pastors, and many other pastors, my friends, who have influenced me by your example, teaching, and counsel.

There have been Christians I have met in other countries who keep serving the Lord, even though they have been threatened and beaten to keep them from continuing their ministry. Thank you for your faithfulness to the Lord.

The person who has influenced me spiritually more than any other person is my wife, Kerry. Kerry lives the Christian life with all her heart and is the same in private that she is in public. During the past several years, I have watched her continue to pursue and fulfill her life's calling to teach and mentor believers, while suffering a deeply emotionally painful trauma. Kerry, you are the most amazing person that I know.

In terms of getting this book out, I am grateful to Kerry for doing initial edits on the manuscript. I am especially grateful to Pastor Steve Blayer, who is one of the finest young pastors I know. He edited the book with careful precision, while maintaining the author's style. I am grateful and amazed at the skill you have brought to *Finishing Strong.* I also want to thank Todd Gearhart, an elder in Pastor Steve's church, who skillfully developed the cover for *Finishing Strong.* Todd has spent many hours helping me get as up to date on tech stuff as possible (a challenging task).

I would be remiss, if I did not mention those who support *KingdomQuest* Ministries financially and those who pray for us. This book would not be possible without you.

I apologize to anyone that I have missed.

Lastly and most importantly, I want to thank the Lord Jesus Christ who looked down at a young man, who had been told he could not do anything right, saved him, and called him to minister to people throughout the world. Lord Jesus, You are awesome, loving, merciful, and just plain amazing! You are worthy of my eternal praise and my life! Glory to your Name!

---

[i] (Voice of the Martyrs Magazine. December 2019. Voice of the Martyrs, Bartlesboro, OK), page 11

[ii] It seems that the devil or Satan had existed with God in heaven, prior to the creation of the earth. Although he held a high position in the angelic order, he was not satisfied with his position and rebelled against God (See Isaiah 14:12-15 and Ezekiel 28:12-19). Satan was cast out of heaven and continued in his rebellion against God to this day.

[iii] The Holy Spirit is the third person of God. God is one (Deut. 6:4), but is made up of three persons: Father, Son and Holy Spirit. This subject is too large to take up in this book.

[iv] The Greek word *ethne*, translated as "nation" means an ethnic group, not geographical nations.

[v] To learn more about Spiritual gifts and how you can discover those God has given to you, see **Becoming You** and **Fully Alive** by this author. Both can be purchased from the author at Shueyconsult@yahoo.com. **Fully Alive** can also be purchased on Kindle.

[vi] These are rounded off statistics based upon the study of the Joshua Project. You can see a record of the groups that are not yet reached by going to joshuaproject.net

[vii] See Balaam's full story in Numbers Chapters 22-24

[viii] See this young man's story in Matthew 19:16-24

[ix] God does not ask everyone to do this, but knew this man would prefer his riches in this life, than following Jesus.

[x] King Solomon's story is told in greater detail in the Books of Samuel, Kings, Chronicles. He is also reputed to have done much of the writing

in the Books of Proverbs, Song of Songs and Ecclesiastes.

[xi] The story of Ananias and Sapphira appears in Acts 5:1-10

[xii] Elijah's story is told in the Books of 1 and 2 Kings

[xiii] You will see most of Jeremiah's story in the Book of Jeremiah

[xiv] The story of this group can be found in the entire Book of Hebrews but especially Heb. 10:32-12:11.

[xv] The Biblical Book of Job describes his difficulties and his encounters with some men who sought to comfort him.

[xvi] You can read about the Apostle Paul in Acts 9-28 and in the many New Testament letters that he wrote. He wrote all the Letters from Romans through Titus and perhaps Hebrews.

[xvii] We read about Peter in the Gospels, Acts and in his letters, 1 and 2 Peter.

[xviii]   https://www.bing.com/search?q=how+did+the+apostle+peter+die&form=EDGSPH&mkt=en-us&httpsmsn=1&msnews=1&rec_search=1&plvar=0&refig=90421f8c77c5468a9f16bb6cb82b0d85&sp=1&ghc=1&qs=AS&pq=how+did+the+apostle+peter+die&sc=4-29&cvid=90421f8c77c5468a9f16bb6cb82b0d85&cc=US&setlang=en-US
ACCESSED 4-25-2020

[xix] https://drkenney.blogspot.come/2014/04/hums-hymn-writers-i-have-decided-t.html accessed 4-23-2020

[xx] Read Pastor Dave Hess's book *Hope Beyond Reason* to see his whole story.

[xxi] David Platt, *Radical* (Colorado Springs: Multnomah Books, 2010), pg. 6

[xxii] http://www.edinburgh2010.org/fileadmin/files/edinburgh2010/files/pdf/Kim-Kwong%20Chan%202009-2-28.pdf
accessed 4-26-2020

[xxiii] K.P.Yohannan, *Never Give Up* (Wills Point, Texas:gfa books a division of GFA World, 2020), p. 75

[xxiv] To see their story read Acts 16, The Letter to the Philippians and 2 Corinthians 8:1-4 (The city of Philippi is located in the province of Macedonia).

[xxv] e-sword.net. Strong's Concordance. Accessed 4-26-2020

[xxvi] Jimmy Larche. *One Way Missionaries*. (Jimmy Larche Abide in Him Devotional http://www.jimmylarche.com/one-way-missionaries-spirit-of-christ-missions/ Accessed 4-28-2020

[xxvii] Majority World is the preferred term for what used to be called "Third World."

[xxviii] Notice that I do not always use names. Because of where they live, I do not want to name them.

[xxix] Read Rifqa's amazing story in: Rifga Bary, *Hiding in the Light* (Colorado Springs, WaterBrook Press, 2015), pg. 90

[xxx] _________ Modern Persecution. (Christianity.com) https://www.christianity.com/church/church-history/timeline/1901-2000/modern-persecution-11630665.html accessed 4-28-2020

[xxxi] John Piper, Spectacular Sins (Wheaton, IL: Good News,2008), 57, Quoted in:
Randy Alcorn, *If God is Good?* (New York, Multnomah, A division of Penguin Random House LLC, 2009), p. 12

[xxxii] Lee Strobel, *The Case for Faith* (Grand Rapid, MI: Zondervan. 2000), 29. Quoted in Alcorn, *If God Is Good*, pg.11

[xxxiii] From chapter one of this book

[xxxiv] I will not print out the Scriptures in this section, so I suggest that you read them for yourself.

[xxxv] My personal theory is that he wanted to take the place of the Lord Jesus.

[xxxvi] Alcorn, *If God Is Good*, p. 238

[xxxvii] See Jonah's story in the Book of Jonah. Jonah did eventually do what God had asked and a great revival broke out.

[xxxviii] If you sincerely prayed that prayer, please contact me at shueyconsult@yahoo.com

[xxxix] Cole Richards, *Will we take our place in God's chain of sacrificial servants and suffering witnesses?* (The Voice of the Martyrs, Bartlesville, OK, May 2020), p.2

[xl] e-sword.net is one of those tools. There are many helps that are free. You can get other translations and helps for minimal fees.

[xli] Adam Clarke, *Commentary on the Bible, Matthew 4:19* from e-sword.net Accessed 5-5-2020

[xlii] Lois Tverberg, *Our Rabbi Jesus blog, The Reality of Disciples and Rabbis* https://ourrabbijesus.com/a-question-about-disciples-rabbis/ Accessed 5-5-2020

[xliii] If you prayed that prayer, I recommend that you get some help to grow in Jesus. I recommend this authors manual: ***Becoming You: How To Discover and Live Out Your Destiny in God***. or John Shuey's ***Fully Alive***. You can get both by contacting John Shuey at shueyconsult@yahoo.com. Fully Alive can also be purchased on Amazon.

[xliv] Many Muslims are having dreams where Jesus appears to them. Many are coming to Christ.

[xlv] _______*Algeria: An Irrepressible Church* (The Voice of the Martyrs, Bartlesville, OK), March 2019, pgs. 6-7

[xlvi] James Strong. Dictionaries of Hebrew and Greek Words taken from Strong's Exhaustive Concordance, logizomai cited in e-sword.net accessed 5-6-2020

[xlvii] Gerhard Kittel, ed., *Theological Dictionary of the New Testament*, trans. Geoffrey W. Bromiley (Grand Rapids, MI; Eerdmans, 1964), 2:681 cited in K. Neill Foster and Paul L. King, *Binding and Loosing* (Camp Hill, PA; Christian Publications, 1998), p. 147

[xlviii] Dr. John Gill, *Exposition of the Entire Bible*, 1 Corinthians 15:43 cited in e-sword.net accessed 5-6-2020

[xlix] Adam Clarke, Commentary on the Bible, 1 Corinthians 15:44 cited in e-sword.net accessed 5-6-2020

[l] Albert Barnes,' *Notes on the Bible,* Revelation 22:4 cited in e-sword.net accessed 5-7-2020

[li] We don't have time to discuss this fully, however, Deuteronomy 6:4 tells us that God is One. Scriptures like John 10:10 tell us that Jesus is one essence with God the Father. Acts 5:3-5 shows that the Holy Spirit and God the Father are one through parallelism. There is much more teaching on this.

[lii] From now on when I will talk about the Holy Spirit praying for us, I mean both Jesus and the Holy Spirit are praying for us.

[liii] Randy Alcorn, *If God is Good* (New York, Crown Publishing, a division of Penguin Random House, printed in US. by Multnomah, 2009), p.473

[liv] No job is secular if we are doing what God wants us to and are seeking God to assist us to use the job and our time spent there to advance His Kingdom.

[lv] John and Kerry Shuey, *Breaking Free to Your Destiny*, self published, copyright 2001

[lvi] College of Prayer International has campuses around the world that stimulate revival and prayer. You can learn more about College of Prayer International at www.collegeofprayer.org

[lvii] Alcorn, p. 410

[lviii] _______*Listening to the Holy Spirit* (Voice of the Martyrs, Bartlesboro, OK, October 2018) , pgs 4-9 Names most likely have been changed to protect those in the story.

[lix] GNT+ citied in e-sword.net, οιδαμεν, accessed 5-12-2020

[lx] Dictionaries of Hebrew and Greek Words taken from Strong's Exhaustive Concordance by James Strong, S.T.D., LL.D., 1890. συνεργέω cited in e-sword.net accessed 5-12-2020

[lxi] Read this story from the life of David in 1 Samuel 27-29

[lxii] Numbers 22:27-30

[lxiii] Acts 9

[lxiv] Randy Alcorn, *If God is Good* (New York; Publish by Multnomah, and imprint of the Crown Publishing Group, a division of Penguin Random House LLC, 2009), From personal correspondence, p. 404

[lxv] You can see the promise repeated to Abraham in Genesis chapters 12 and 15

[lxvi] Alcorn, *If God is Good*, p. 410

[lxvii] Nick Vujicic, "A Remarkable Story of God's Grace," Life Without Limbs, www.lifewithoutlimbs,org/about-nick-vujicic.php Cited in Alcorn If God is Good, p.395

[lxviii] C.S. Lewis, *The Problem of Pain* (New York: Macmillan, 1962), p. 92 Cited in Randy Alcorn, *If God is Good* (New York; Publish by Multnomah, and imprint of the Crown Publishing Group, a division of Penguin Random House LLC, 2009),p. 419

[lxix] C.S. Lewis, pg. 93, cited in Alcorn, p. 393

[lxx] John Hick, Evil and the God of Love (New York: Macmillan, 1966), p. 259 cited in Alcorn, p.392-393

[lxxi] Dictionaries of Hebrew and Greek Words taken from Strong's Exhaustive Concordance by James Strong, S.T.D., LL.D., 1890. καυχάομαι cited in e-sword.net accessed 5-14-2020

[lxxii] Strongs ὑπομονή, cited in e-sword.net accessed 5-14-2020

[lxxiii] Strongs, δοκιμή, cited in e-sword.net accessed 5-14-2020

[lxxiv] Strong's, ἐλπίς, cited in e-sword.net accessed 5-14-2020

[lxxv] Alcorn, pgs. 400-401

[lxxvi] Alcorn, pgs. 393-394

[lxxvii] Strong's, τέλειος cited in e-sword.net accessed 5-14-2020

[lxxviii] You can read the story of this long imprisonment and the amazing things that happened in Acts 21:27 to the end of the Book of Acts.

[lxxix] I want to mention that the church did have a second parsonage, which they allowed us to live in until I graduated and found a position. In addition, the youth pastor that they hired did a phenomenal job.

[lxxx] Alcorn, quote and story on page 429

[lxxxi] I heard Lance make this comment at a conference at Christ Community Church in Camp Hill, PA

[lxxxii] Jim L. Wilson, *Six True Stories of Sacrifice* (Reuters News Service, 6-24-1997) Illustration by Jim L. Wilson cited in https://sermons.faithlife.com/sermons/80703-six-true-stories-of-sacrifice accessed

5-18-2020

[lxxxiii] James Strong, *Dictionaries of Hebrew and Greek Words taken from Strong's Exhaustive Concordance by James Strong, S.T.D., LL.D., 1890.* φείδομαι, "spared means abstain" cited in e-sword.net 5-18-2020

[lxxxiv] Some versions say 70 times 7.

[lxxxv] Her name has been changed and we cannot mention her country.

[lxxxvi] John and Kerry Shuey, *Breaking Free to Your Destiny* (Self published-KingdomQuest Ministries), 2001. The workbook can be ordered by emailing: shueyconsult@yahoo.com.

[lxxxvii] James Strong, *Dictionaries of Hebrew and Greek Words taken from Strongn's Exhaustive Concordance by James Strong, S.T.D. LLD, 1890,* πικρία, cited in e-sword.net accessed 5-18-2020

[lxxxviii] James Strong, *Dictionaries of Hebrew and Greek Words taken from Strongn's Exhaustive Concordance by James Strong, S.T.D. LLD, 1890,* φέρω, cited in e-sword.net accessed 5-19-2020

[lxxxix] To learn more see *Fully Alive and Becoming* You by John Shuey. Both can be purchased by emailing to shueyconsult@yahoo.com. *Fully Alive* can be purchased at Amazon.

[xc] The Lockman Foundation, *New American Standard Bible* (Moody Press, Chicago, 1960, 1962, 1963, 1971, 1972, 1973, 1975), p.1057, note in center of page for Acts 19:19

[xci] Paul's letter to the Ephesians is called the Epistle to the Ephesians

[xcii] James Strong, *Dictionaries of Hebrew and Greek Words taken from Strong's Exhaustive Concordance by James Strong, S.T.D., LL.D., 1890.* μεταμορφόω cited in e-sword.net accessed 5-21-2020

[xciii] James Strong, *Dictionaries of Hebrew and Greek Words taken from Strong's Exhaustive Concordance by James Strong, S.T.D., LL.D., 1890.* ἀνακαίνωσις cited in e-sword.net accessed 5-21-2020

[xciv] Silvoso, Ed. *That None Should Perish* (Ventura, California: Regal Books, Copyright 1994), page 166

[xcv] http://www.navigators.org/us/resources/illustrations/items/The%20Word%20Hand cited on https://www.josh-hunt.com/2011/03/11/the-navigators-hand-illustration/ accessed 5-21-2020

[xcvi] A couple of organizations that may help you here are Navigators at https://www.navigators.org and Cru at https://www.cru.org

[xcvii] James Strong, *Dictionaries of Hebrew and Greek Words taken from Strong's Exhaustive Concordance* by James Strong, S.T.D., LL.D., 1890.

φρουρέω cited in e-sword.net accessed 5-22-2020

[xcviii] We will talk more about spiritual authority in Chapter Twelve.

[xcix] Names in this chapter have been changed for privacy purposes.

[c] Both the book *Fully Alive* and the manual *Becoming You* talk of the gifts in greater detail. These can be ordered at shueyconsult@ yahoo.com or *Fully Alive* can be ordered on Amazon.

[ci] James Strong *Dictionaries of Hebrew and Greek Words taken from Strong's Exhaustive Concordance by James Strong, S.T.D., LL.D., 1890.* ἐξουσία cited in e-sword.net accessed 5-26-2020

[cii] _______*The Amplified Bible Large Print* (Grand Rapids, MI, Zondervan Publishing House and Lockman Foundation, 1987), p. 1422 Matthew 16:19

[ciii] Paul King from "A Believer with Authority: The Impact of the Life and Ministry of John A. Macmillan" This is King's doctoral dissertation cited in K. Neill Forster and Paul L. King Binding and Loosing (Camp Hill, PA, Christian Publications, 1998) p. 246-247

[civ] *Breaking Free* can be ordered from John Shuey at the email in note ii.

[cv] Albert Barnes' *Notes on the Bible* Romans 8:35 - cited in e-sword.net accessed 5-26-2020

[cvi] Barnes, Romans 8:35 - cited in e-sword.net accessed 5-26-2020

[cvii] Adam Clarke, *Adam Clarke's Commentary on the Bible* Romans 8:35 - cited in e-sword.net accessed 5-26-2020

[cviii] It is implied that 1/3rd of angels fell with Lucifer, who became Satan. Most, myself included, believe that this explains the origin of demons. This would make demons equal, at least in creation to angels.

[cix] _______Traditional Wedding Vows for Your Ceremony https://www.marthastewartweddings.com/618155/traditional-wedding-vows accessed 5-28-2020

[cx] James Strong, *Dictionaries of Hebrew and Greek Words taken from Strong's Exhaustive Concordance by James Strong, S.T.D., LL.D., 1890.* ἀνίημι and ἐγκαταλείπω cited in e-sword.net accessed 5-28-2020

[cxi] By revelation, I mean that God has made Himself real to us in a way that may have only be information to us in the past. We may have known it intellectually, but now this character trait of God is etched in our inner being.

[cxii] Our manual *Becoming You* can help with all of these. Order at shueyconsult@yahoo.com

www.ingramcontent.com/pod-product-compliance
Lightning Source LLC
Chambersburg PA
CBHW061527120726
48001CB00004B/1422